Material Girls

Material Girls

*Making Sense of Feminist
Cultural Theory*

Suzanna Danuta Walters

UNIVERSITY OF CALIFORNIA PRESS
BERKELEY LOS ANGELES LONDON

University of California Press
Berkeley and Los Angeles, California

University of California Press, Ltd.
London, England

©1995 by
The Regents of the University of California

Library of Congress Cataloging-in-Publication Data

Walters, Suzanna Danuta.
    Material girls: making sense of feminist cultural theory /
Suzanna Danuta Walters.
        p.   cm.
    Includes bibliographical references and index.
    ISBN 0-520-08977-4 (alk. paper). — ISBN 0-520-08978-2 (pbk.:
alk. paper)
    1. Culture.   2. Feminist criticism.   3. Women in popular culture.
4. Feminist theory.   I. Title.
HM101.W225   1995
305.42'01—dc20   94-29007
                                                               CIP

Printed in the United States of America
9 8 7 6 5 4 3 2 1

The paper used in this publication meets the minimum requirements
of American National Standard for Information Sciences—Permanence
of Paper for Printed Library Materials, ANSI Z39.48-1984.

To feminists everywhere:

"Fasten your seatbelts. It's going to be a bumpy night."
—Bette Davis as Margo Channing
in *All About Eve*

Contents

Acknowledgments

A book on feminist cultural theory necessarily relies on a community of women who provide the social and political context for feminist theoretical work. I want to thank Fina Bathrick who, as always, has helped out in innumerable ways. She is a wonderful friend and mentor. Lynn Chancer—friend, comrade, critic—offered helpful criticism as usual, even as we kvetched together over deadlines and professorial angst. Ben Agger (not a woman but a good feminist nonetheless), who first published an article of mine on feminist cultural theory, continues to be supportive and encouraging. Annie Gibeau and Diane Lopez remain the best of friends, providing the love and support fifteen years of shared sisterhood brings; knowing that they are in my life is itself empowering. I would also like to thank my colleagues at Colorado College and Georgetown University, particularly Margi Duncombe, Adrienne Seward, Tom Lindblade, Esther Redmount, and the members of the women's studies community at Georgetown. C. Margaret Hall, director of women's studies at Georgetown and colleague in the sociology department, has been an invaluable friend and mentor—her support and encouragement have been truly inspiring. Leona Fisher, of women's studies and English at Georgetown, has also been

exceedingly supportive and made me feel instantly wel-
come at Georgetown. Molly Andrews helpfully commented
on versions of this book and provided the requisite silli-
ness necessary for serious scholarship. Gwyn Kirk, ecofem-
inist extraordinaire, always had time for a glass of wine
and a chat about the vicissitudes of feminist theory and
politics. Nancy Knipe's love of movies made for wonderful hours of filmgoing and critical reflection. Amy Robinson generously pitched in at the last, anxiety-filled
moments. My mother, as always, provides both emotional
and intellectual support. She remains my favorite material girl, always pushing me to write accessibly and to make
my ideas known. And she devours popular culture with a
vigor even exceeding my own!

Many students over the years have helped enormously
in clarifying the important questions for feminist cultural
theory. In particular, I would like to thank my research
assistants, Courtney Jackson and Vanessa Landegger, for
their diligent work and always questioning minds. Carol
Gangnath was a big help during the last few weeks. I would
also like to thank my editor, Naomi Schneider, and the rest
of the production team at the University of California Press,
particularly project editor Dore Brown.

Most of all, however, I want to thank all the feminist cultural theorists whose work has meant so much to me, particularly Jackie Byars, Teresa de Lauretis, Jane Gaines,
Christine Gledhill, E. Ann Kaplan, Annette Kuhn, Judith
Mayne, Tania Modleski, Laura Mulvey, Janice Radway,
Judith Williamson, and many others. Their pioneering
work has inspired me and continues to enrich the field.

Introduction
On Outlaw Women and Single Mothers

The title of this book is, of course, a reference to Madonna's hit song of several years ago. Madonna is a likely starting point for a discussion of feminism and cultural theory, for she has re-created herself as image many times over: from sluttish, pouty boy-toy to Marilyn Monroe glamor queen to every nun's worst nightmare. Perhaps Madonna's most outrageous incarnation, after a brief and obviously half-hearted attempt at marriage, was as trendy gay girl with fellow postmodern bon vivant Sandra Bernhard—thereby introducing lesbianism as fun into the *National Enquirer*. After being banned from music television (MTV) for her erotic, mildly sadomasochistic video *Justify Your Love*, Madonna spoke out against censorship and against the real violence of male-defined visual imagery. Her most recent efforts at sex and self-promotion included the publication of her book *Sex*, featuring photos of the material girl in her kinkiest materiality and accompanying text elaborating her fantasies through her dominatrix of an alter ego, Dita.

Accompanying Madonna's own elaboration of super-stardom has been a sustained effort—by the mass media and academics alike—to continually produce and reproduce this cultural icon. Madonna circulates constantly in the cultural practices of everyday life, from lurid *National Enquirer* exposés to the serious cultural scholarship that has been dubbed "Madonna-ology" and that has produced at least one major academic text devoted to Madonna in all her (meta) incarnations.[1]

In these academic writings, Madonna (Figure 1) is understood variously as an empowering icon of feminist sensibility, a campy cult figure for both gay men and gay women, a personification of commodity capitalism and its capacity to make human beings into objects for sale and circulation, and a player with codes and conventions. Many critics see her as all these things: the postmodern Circe herself, embodying all the contradictions of a society fascinated by fame, ambivalent about sexuality, hostile toward women. Perhaps, as Shelagh Young notes, "the problem of Madonna for feminists was that she transgressed both the category of the feminine and of the feminist. Madonna's self-determinedly aggressive sexual presentation certainly undermined the conventional understanding of feminine sexuality as essentially passive, but in what way does this engage with feminist politics?"[2] The ambiguity of Madonna's self-presentation (Is she putting us on? Is she mocking the male gaze or willfully giving in to it? Is she whore or madonna, or both, or neither?) points to the already overdetermined status of representing woman in popular culture. In other words, it ain't easy being a girl.

The figure of Madonna is emblematic of the confused way women are represented in popular culture. We must reckon with the complicated and contradictory nature of images in our culture. It is too simplistic to state that there

Figure 1.   Madonna in her 1990 Blonde Ambition tour mode.
(Photo courtesy of Photofest)

are "bad" images that produce "bad" attitudes and behaviors; unfortunately, the situation is more complex than that. Different audiences may interpret the same images in various ways. One group's "negative" image may be another's source of empowerment, and the reception of Madonna is a prime example of this complexity.

Two other cultural "moments" of the early 1990s allow me to elaborate what the stakes are for women studying representation and for women as represented objects in our culture. One of the hit films of 1991, *Thelma and Louise* (Figure 2), is a helpful opening for a book on feminism and culture. A female buddy film, it takes us on the (highly stylized, Western) road with Thelma, a homebound housewife, and Louise, a hardbitten waitress, as they attempt to elude the law after Louise has killed Thelma's would-be rapist. To assess such a film is no easy task and forcefully proves the limitations of a purely textual analysis (an analysis focusing solely on the actual representation) and the need for what I will be calling a feminist contextualism or, more generally, a feminist cultural studies.

The story of the impact of *Thelma and Louise* runs something like this: a film is produced by an acclaimed action-film director (Ridley Scott) and a first-time screenwriter (Callie Khouri) and sets off a torrent of debate. It is alternately read—by the popular press and the popular media— as an angry, violent, "man-bashing" piece of radical feminist propaganda, or as a brave film about feminist consciousness and resistance. Male film critics froth at the mouth, screaming at the director and screenwriter for promoting female violence in response to male violence. Female critics respond, largely defending the film and rationalizing its "excesses" as a legitimate response to male violence and sexual assault. They focus on the generic aspects of the film, its encoding of feminist values within the traditionally male road movie/buddy motif. They praise the two stars, Geena Davis and Susan Sarandon, for their sensitivity and insight. The actresses hit the covers of *Time* and *Newsweek*. Bumper stickers and buttons begin to appear: "Thelma & Louise Finishing School." To "Thelma and Louise" someone becomes a verb. Editorials appear in reputable papers like

Figure 2. From one-night stand to two-fisted empowerment, Thelma and Louise ride the ambiguous road to liberated adventures and tragic endings. (Metro Goldwyn Mayer, 1991; photos courtesy of Museum of Modern Art Film Stills Archive)

the *New York Times*, debating the film and its "message." As is true of so many "explosive" media moments, we can learn more from the contentious public discourse that surrounded the film than from the film itself.

With *Thelma and Louise*, we are faced with a situation in which a film becomes part of a larger discourse on representations of women in Hollywood, male violence, female responses to violence, and so on. *Thelma and Louise*, like more and more of our cultural output, became a signal moment, a "symptomatic" text—much as the film *Fatal Attraction* had been a few years earlier. As feminist critic Sharon Willis notes: "Like *Fatal Attraction* (1987), *Thelma and Louise* plugged into ambient anxieties about sexual difference, and men's and women's places as organized by the 'battle of the sexes.' And like *Fatal Attraction, Thelma and Louise* troubled borderlines that contemporary popular critical discourse continues to code as fragile: those between art and life, fantasy and agency, cinematic fiction and the life stories we tell ourselves."[3] The movie became part of a "great debate" over whether it was "evil man-bashing or a liberating fantasy."[4] The range of opinions on *Thelma and Louise* was actually quite broad, spreading from "it's just fantasy, relax" to "it's just a road movie, and therefore violent like the male films of that genre," to "it's feminist and progressive" to "it's violent and male-bashing." One critic even claimed it was "fascistic."[5] Nonetheless, the lines were often drawn between angry (usually male) commentators and their exultant (usually female) counterparts.

John Robinson, writing in the *Boston Globe*, spoke for many male critics when he claimed that "the movie makes men out to be either rapists or accessories to rape."[6] His attack was telling, as he argued that the film is an example of "male-bashing" that, strangely enough, signals the end of feminism: "Male bashing, once the sport of hairy women in denim jackets and combat boots, has flushed like toxic waste into the cultural mainstream with the vengeance fantasy 'Thelma & Louise.' . . . And it makes clear that equality is no longer—if it ever was—the goal of the New Girl Network. It says domination or death are the only feminist alternatives. It says, inadvertently, that feminism is dying, not with a bang but with a bashing."[7] In this reading, the film became a reference point for a pop version of feminism. The critic here created a narrative of "man-bashing" by constructing a (revisionist) history of the women's movement, specifically encoding this history so as to suggest its lesbian context. John Leo, writing in *U.S. News and World Report*, contributed a similar analysis, linking the film to his larger anxiety over the women's movement: "The scene is set in the Southwest, but the real landscape is that of writer Andrea Dworkin and the most alienated radical feminists. All males in the movie exist only to betray, ignore, sideswipe, penetrate or arrest our heroines."[8] What is significant is that feminism became the frame through which this film was analyzed, and, as a result, the complexities of feminism and feminist demands for serious structural change were often displaced in a glib focus on "male-bashing."[9]

Indeed, many critics took the opportunity to rail against feminism and its "male-bashing" excesses, claiming reverse sexism was at work in the film: "Any movie that went as far out of its way to trash women as this female chauvinist sow of a film does to trash men would be universally, and justifiably, condemned."[10]

In the right-wing *National Review*, John Simon went even further in his attack on feminism, claiming Thelma "asked for it" when she attempted to leave the bar and get some air: "Provocative as she is, she gets not air, but attempted rape."[11] In a consistently irrational review, Simon went on to assert the possibility of, as he put it, "an emotional merger": "Are these women, consciously or unconsciously, in love with each other? Is this perhaps not just a feminist but also a lesbian feminist movie?"[12]

Other critics, often women, urged the boys to "lighten up." "Really, boys. Calm yourselves," said Diane White of the *Boston Globe*. White argued, with no small amount of contradiction, first, that the film is just a fantasy, a *film* after all, and second, that she understood the desire to fight back against male violence.[13]

Mary Cantwell was one of the few writers to place the film in the context of the real violence women face every day. Recounting the true story of a group of women college students harassed by a group of young men while on vacation, Cantwell wrote: "If Thelma and Louise's ride sometimes seems as mythic as the flight of Icarus, the pressures that propel them are not. Anyone who doubts that need only be young, female and renting a cottage on Cape Cod to be shown otherwise."[14]

In an interview with *People* magazine, star Geena Davis made a strong statement on the treatment of women in film: "Let's get real here for a second. Ninety-nine percent of all other movies are about women either having shallow, one-dimensional caricature parts or they're being mutilated, skinned, slaughtered, abused and exploited with their clothes off. Even if this film did convey some horrible man-bashing message—'Let's us gals all get guns and kill all the men'—it couldn't even begin to make up for all the anti-woman movies people don't even talk about."[15]

Yet even many of the critics who loved the film (and there were many, perhaps even more than the ones who found it "fascistic") were unable to pass up the opportunity to take pot shots at feminism: "Whether or not the women's movement sacrifices moral advantage in this film that allows women to do some of the violent things men have been doing unquestioned for decades is not the main issue, as some orthodox feminist critics claim. In this age of potentially suffocating political correctness, it's worth remembering that a work of art is not a moral tract."[16]

In an interesting piece in *Time*, Margaret Carlson asserted that the film is not feminist at all:

> Yet for all the pleasure the film gives women moviegoers who want to see the worst of the opposite sex get what's coming to them, it can hardly be called a woman's movie or one with a feminist sensibility. As a bulletin from the front in the battle of the sexes, *Thelma & Louise* sends the message that little ground has been won. For these two women, feminism never happened. Thelma and Louise are so trapped that the only way for them to get away for more than two days is to go on the lam. They become free but only wildly, self-destructively so—free to drive off the ends of the earth. They are also free to behave like—well, men. For all the talk that *Thelma & Louise* is the first major female buddy movie, it is more like a male buddy movie with two women plunked down in the starring roles. The turning point of Thelma's character rests on one of the most enduring and infuriating male myths in the culture: the only thing an unhappy woman needs is good sex to make everything all right. . . . Thelma is transformed, more confident and buoyant than she has ever been, reducing her angst to the simplistic notion that she was stuck with a husband who was insufficiently accomplished in the bedroom.[17]

I, too, have difficulty defining this film as feminist. After the attempted rape, Thelma picks up a man on the highway and has a night of wild and passionate sex in which, we are led to believe, she has her first orgasm. Not only is this event troubling, falling as it does on the heels of sexual violence, but it is the narrative moment when the tables turn on the relationship between the two women and Thelma, formerly unable to manage anything, becomes the aggressive, strong manager of their ensuing escapades. In other words, all she needed was a "good fuck" to awaken the woman in her and empower her to act on her own behalf.

Even the killing of the would be rapist, though a moment of powerful and visceral retribution, is apparently motivated by Louise's own earlier experience of sexual violence, rather than by a more generalized inclination to avenge women. This angle personalizes the issue of male violence and women's responses to it and stresses individual experience over collective history as the motivating force for women's empowerment.[18] Not exactly a message of self-empowerment or female *collective* empowerment, this film's exciting focus on the relationship between two women is made narratively possible by male sexuality.

To understand this film's explosion onto the cultural scene, we must not limit ourselves to that textual and narrative analysis which, while perhaps a more accurate reading of the structure of the film, does not provide much insight into the way it became a "symptomatic" text—a text that spoke to larger cultural anxieties and issues surrounding women, male violence, and representation. Indeed, the incessant dialogue about this film points not only to the power of feminism and the anxieties women's independence evokes but to the power of the backlash against that very feminism that was so brilliantly charted by Susan Faludi in her bestselling book *Backlash*. Clearly, as film critic Manohla Dargis noted, "*Thelma & Louise* strikes a nerve—as the cover of *Time* announced—because it's about power, *female power*. Released the same day the Supreme Court's gag-rule made news, the film, with its complex and contradictory messages about women, violence, and power, certainly couldn't be more timely."[19]

About a year later, Vice President Dan Quayle (in the

midst of a vitriolic election year) attacked the television sitcom *Murphy Brown*. The lead character, television anchorwoman Murphy Brown (played by Candice Bergen), had ended a successful season with the birth of her child. In a speech made in San Francisco in May 1992 to the Commonwealth Club, Quayle ranted against this portrayal of single parenthood, claiming the show and its star took a cavalier attitude toward parenting and presented bad role models for young viewers. Speaking after the Los Angeles riots, Quayle bemoaned the sorry state of moral values and individual responsibility, claiming that "it doesn't help matters when prime-time TV has Murphy Brown, a character who supposedly epitomizes today's intelligent, highly paid, professional woman, mocking the importance of fathers by bearing a child alone, and calling it just another lifestyle choice."[20] Quayle's speech became the spark that ignited what one could call the "family values" debate that raged in the newspapers and visual media for months and that became a salient topic for election-year speechifying and political campaigning.

From Johnny Carson to David Letterman ("Dan Quayle's top ten other complaints about television") to literally hundreds of newspaper articles, television shows, and radio broadcasts, this speech saturated the cultural landscape. The *New York Daily News*'s front-page headline "Quayle to Murphy Brown: You Tramp!" was only one such (amusing) moment. The Quayle remarks provoked not only a response on the television show itself, but endless editorials, articles, television commentaries—from *Time* to the *New York Times*, from *CBS This Morning* to the *Wall Street Journal* (taking the opportunity to trash the media for its liberal bent).[21] In true postmodern fashion, the speech again recirculated when in the opening *Murphy Brown* show of the next season the title character "spoke" to her accuser. The media–"real world" interaction intensified as Dan Quayle (dutifully covered by television newspeople) watched the episode with a group of single African-American parents in Washington, D.C.

Even sober columnists commented on the curious interpenetration of media and life:

> If there was still a distinction between politics and entertainment in America before Monday night's episode of "Murphy Brown," there did not seem to be one afterward. In the special one-hour episode, an exhausted Ms. Brown, played by Candice Bergen, returned home with her newborn son to find the Vice President on TV news—shown in actual news clips—criticizing her. Livid, she returned to her job to deliver a long, moralistic attack against the Vice President on her television-show-within-a-television-show.[22]

Quayle went on to send the fictional son of the fictional Murphy Brown a stuffed elephant (symbol of the Republican party) and to air radio announcements for the television series, using another popular culture reference ("Not!" from *Wayne's World*) to describe his favorite show.

Even those who thought the vice president's comments ill-advised and rather stupid found themselves agreeing with him on the "problem" of single-parent households. John Leo, who said, "I think Dan Quayle is a proven nincompoop," still found the "message" accurate: "If the message is that family disintegration and the dramatic rise of single-parent families are a major social disaster for this country, then the message is clearly correct." He went on, quoting sociologist Amitai Etzioni and others (such as former assistant secretary of education Chester Finn), to declare that, in Etzioni's words, "single parenting is harmful to children."[23]

Right-wing pundit Barbara Dafoe Whitehead wrote an

early piece (before her infamous "Dan Quayle Was Right" piece in the *Atlantic*) in which she condemned the "glamorizing" of single motherhood and argued that "the single-mother-by-choice story assaults the very foundation of child well-being. The plain truth is that every child needs both a mother and a father."[24] Douglas Besharov of the right-wing American Enterprise Institute took the opportunity to focus attention on what he saw as a distinction between those "good" single mothers (divorced) and those "bad" ones (unwed teenage mothers) and to argue for "a clearer understanding of the divergent values that underlie each behavior."[25]

Some writers in mainstream publications managed to put a more revealing light on the incident. Ellen Snortland, writing in the *Los Angeles Times*, said that "'traditional family values' is a right-wing euphemism for 'a white family where Daddy's the boss.' . . . Our country's government is not pro-motherhood, or even pro-parenthood. It's anti-choice, pro-married and in favor of 'traditional' motherhood because the guys in government want the old fairy-tale days back."[26] Still other commentators took the opportunity to speak of women's lack of real choices in life.[27] Many leapt to the defense of single mothers, and none more eloquently than Dorothy Gilliam, longtime columnist for the *Washington Post*. She condemned Quayle's scapegoating of single mothers and declared that "this pseudo-dialogue is not about family values, the values of the diverse families that make up the United States."[28] The debate about "family values" did not end when the initial furor over the remarks subsided; indeed, this phrase has now become part of our contemporary cultural vocabulary.

These two incidents are only a small sampling of our media culture, not really special ones, yet emblematic of the depth of media saturation in modern American society. They illustrate central tenets of the kind of feminist cultural theory I will be elaborating in this book. First, we cannot possibly understand either of these events simply by watching *Thelma and Louise* and *Murphy Brown*. This, for me, exemplifies the remarkable level of intertextuality in the contemporary social and cultural environment. We cannot simply "read" these events as discrete texts of culture, as many formalist critics so elegantly do. The meanings of these narratives exist not only in the actual narrative moment of the cultural articulation, but in the vast and complex circuit of articulations that both precede and follow the localized event.

The "event" of the birth of a child "out of wedlock" is only a salient event if a social context exists in which single parenthood, working mothers, and abortion have become the favored stomping ground for the patriarchal right wing. This is not to say that the episode would not have incited questions and discussions were we living in a more hospitable time for women. Nevertheless, it is important to note that, twenty years earlier, the television character Maude took the option (abortion) that the producer of *Murphy Brown* claimed her star could not take in this era of backlash and antiabortion fervor. Indeed, the producer of *Murphy Brown*, Diane English, responded to Quayle's speech with just this context in mind: "If the Vice President thinks it's disgraceful for an unmarried woman to bear a child and if he believes that a woman cannot adequately raise a child without a father, then he'd better make sure abortion remains safe and legal."[29] Quayle's ranting was not just accidental; it was made possible by a context in which "the family" has been a phrase captured by conservative politicians and used as a barometer of social morality.

But the context extends beyond the political discourses that embrace the event and construct it in new and more all-encompassing ways. Indeed, one must pay attention not only to the competing "extratextual" discourses around this particular show, but also to the competing modes of spectatorship and how actual viewers watch the event and then enter into the circuit of discourses as they read Quayle's remarks in the morning paper or see a debate on "family values" on *Nightline*. Women and men all over the country debated both *Thelma and Louise* and *Murphy Brown*, and these debates were immediately informed by the outpouring of a highly public discussion, which drew on both other representations (for example, *Thelma and Louise* in relation to other buddy movies, such as *Butch Cassidy and the Sundance Kid*) and preexisting discourses (for example, about the politics of the family and the women's movement). Attacks on single mothers are not new, and odes to the nuclear family have a long history in American culture; the significance lies in the way this particular representation picked up and then restructured and renegotiated these familial discourses.

What struck me most about the subsequent fervor that surrounded the airing of the *Murphy Brown* episode was that it seemed to have nothing to do with the show I viewed that fateful evening. I, too, was disturbed by the show and found it represented problematic values to American youth. While Quayle castigated Murphy for her errant ways, implying not so subtly that she was too feminist, I wanted to castigate her for her very *lack* of feminism, for her obsequiousness in the face of traditional definitions of maternity. Indeed, I found the last image of that episode, which shows Murphy in bed holding the newborn boy and singing "You Make Me Feel Like a Natural Woman," nauseating (Figure 3). Hardly emblematic of female self-definition and empowerment, the rancid words to that song ("now I know just what was wrong with me") placed

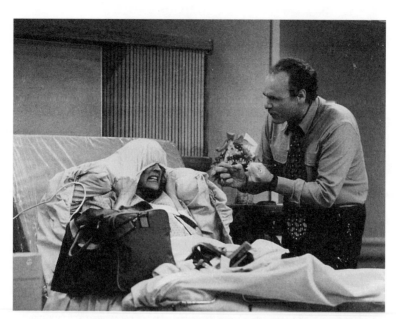

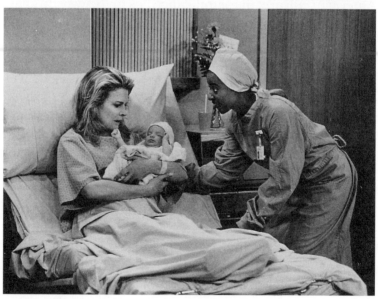

Figure 3.   Murphy Brown has paroxysms of incompetence at delivery, only to be rewarded with a son who makes her feel "like a natural woman." (CBS, 1991–92, photos courtesy of Photofest)

Murphy firmly on the side of transformative and innate motherhood—birth as a woman's most significant moment, as transcendent, as inevitable.

The entire depiction of both the birth and the previous episodes of the pregnancy portrays an intelligent, successful, able woman suddenly flummoxed by the possibility of birth. A less than oblique jab at professional women as naive and hysterical little girls underneath all the bluster, this show pays homage to feminism without fundamentally challenging the bedrock assumptions of patriarchal culture. At the delivery, Murphy has no community of women surrounding her and supporting her, but rather is forced to settle for her housepainter, whose sheer presence in her life constitutes a meaningful relationship. The absence of any significant women friends not only rings false for so many of us, but further paints the picture of successful, tough, funny Murphy as really a sad, alone, incompetent little girl at heart whose maternity points out to her "what was wrong" all along.

Yet my reading of these two cultural moments as questionable if not antifeminist bears little on the cultural reception and experience of them. As we have seen, these specific representations never exist in isolation. As long as male critics construct *Thelma and Louise* as a man-bashing feminist diatribe, feminist critics (and, one might argue, women viewers as well) are hard-pressed to present a more nuanced and complex view of the meaning of that film. As long as the vice president sees fit to pronounce on "family values" through the medium of a television sitcom, we (both the general viewing public and feminist critics) must engage with that discourse, as much as we try to push it beyond those simplistic and misogynist moorings. So, of course, I found myself defending both *Thelma and Louise* and *Murphy Brown*, unable to discover a way to be critical and supportive at the same time, given the prevailing social context of backlash and antifeminism.

Madonna, *Thelma and Louise*, *Murphy Brown*—all are central images in the construction of female identity and ideas about women's lives and women's options. Any good feminist criticism must contend with these "symptomatic" images, yet must always place these images in a context that helps us to understand why and how they *become* symptomatic and, further, what the implications are for feminist possibilities embodied in the discourses that swirl so furiously around these cultural icons.

The Evolution of Cultural Studies

In this era where the image rules and the referent fades further and further into a fond memory, the need for cultural analysis and critique becomes profoundly urgent. But where does feminism fit in? Do women have a particular relationship to cultural imagery? What, in fact, is the relationship between *women* as material, historical beings and *woman*—that contradictory and frustrating image of ourselves that is represented in popular culture? Finally, the question that concerns us here: How can we begin to develop a specifically *feminist* cultural theory? The question is not an idle one, or simply resolved by the "add women and stir" method of most cultural analyses.

Indeed, the last fifteen years have witnessed a phenomenal growth in the area of feminism and representation, traversing all types of cultural artifacts, including film, television, and advertising.[30] Literary criticism, in particular, has responded to a growing feminist movement and the introduction of women's studies into the academy, so that we can now almost point to an alternative feminist literary "canon."[31] The language of feminist film criticism— particularly in its Lacanian versions[32]—has entered into the critical vocabulary of film theorists on both sides of the Atlantic, and has found a home within film schools and media courses. In recent years feminist critics have examined that peculiarly home-based and ubiquitous medium of television and are beginning to explore the complex relations between television families and "real" families, between soap opera and everyday life. Women's magazines, long ignored and trivialized, have now been recognized as the powerful forces they are in shaping and structuring commonsense understandings of femininity. The everpresent figure of the advertising image, which appears as

so much "background" information, has been deconstructed and criticized both for its portrayal of women
and for the consumerist ethos it so vividly and successfully promotes.

There is also a larger context, however: the context of
the "media society" itself. As early as 1967 Guy Debord put
forward the by now accepted postmodern claim that we
live in a world increasingly defined by the image; we live
in a "society of the spectacle," as Debord titled his book.
In more recent years, the French postmodern theorist Jean
Baudrillard has expanded on this theme and stressed the
dominance of "simulacra" in a world where everything is
reduced to an appearance, a simulation of the real which
does not exist anymore.

Whether postmodern or simply modern, most cultural
critics have acceded to the claim that our world is increasingly marked by the presence of communications technologies in all areas of life: from the family clustered
around its "entertainment center" complete with color television (with all-night cable channels), remote-control
video, and compact disc player to the student or business-
person staring into the green screen of a home computer,
the new technologies are an ever-present part of American reality. Whether one sees these phenomena as simply
an extension of the logic of consumer capitalism, or as a
fundamentally new shift requiring new theories and political alignments, is itself a subject of much debate.

Yet the sheer growth in new media technologies and their
increasing presence in everyday life are inescapable realities, brought home to many of us by the election of Ronald
Reagan in 1980, when an old "B" movie actor became the
first truly media-savvy U.S. president. It is no accident that
the widely read cartoon *Doonesbury* chose to parody Reagan by placing him as a sort of addled android filling the

television screen of which he seems to be an integral part. Arguably, no election has been the same since.

Thus, it can surely be no coincidence that, as this media frame grows increasingly larger, encompassing more and more areas of social practice, an outpouring of cultural critique of all stripes emerges from even those formerly concerned with the most orthodox of endeavors. On the left, this can be seen as a shift (still in process) from a Frankfurt School[33] condemnation of mass culture to a more tentative and perhaps even optimistic version of cultural resistance and political possibilities. Since the Frankfurt School declared mass culture to be the last decadent gasp of a culture in decay, numerous attempts have been made to reevaluate popular culture and to challenge this view of it (shared by many conservative and mainstream theorists along with the marxists Theodor Adorno and Max Horkheimer) as debased and necessarily aiding in the wholesale reproduction of capitalism and its associated repressions. Popular culture came to be seen as a legitimate area of social analysis that was not simply reducible to a variety of brainwashing metaphors and terms of denigration. New methods and analytic frameworks that were responsive to the specifics of *mass* culture—as opposed to "high culture" categories and values—were needed to fully understand the scope and meaning of "the popular." Laura Kipnis[34] may be right when she asserts that "mass culture" has now become the privileged subject of left-wing academia. As courses in popular culture appear on the university campuses and reputable academics turn from their dusty books to expostulate on the bewildering popularity of *The Cosby Show* and the meanings of Madonna, cultural studies emerges as a popular form itself.

In any case, it is surely no longer possible to understand the media as somehow "outside" society or an adjunct to "larger" social concerns. One could argue that the media have so inserted themselves into the everyday life of most Americans (indeed, most people) that they have come to construct our sense of what it means to live in the (post)-modern world. This new emphasis on mass cultural criticism is, for many theorists, itself indicative of the move to a postmodern culture: Kipnis notes that "the shift from a refusal to an embrace of the popular in theoretical discourse marks a break between modernism and postmodernism."[35] The media *are* everywhere, and as such can no longer be relegated to secondary status in any critical analysis of contemporary society.

Feminist critics have been quick to point out that the representation of *women* in this media-saturated society is particularly fraught with contradictions and dilemmas. For it is women who more often than not are the "imaged" in our culture. In this society of the spectacle, it is women's bodies that are the spectacle upon which representation occurs; it is women's bodies that are "represented as the negative term of sexual differentiation, spectacle-fetish or specular image . . . woman is constituted as the ground of representation, the looking glass held up to man."[36] This is true not simply for the most visible manifestations of, say, pornography, but for the innocuous advertising image and the mundane television movie of the week as well. Women's bodies sell cars, beer, and laundry detergent; women's loves and lives sell soap opera fantasies; women's fears and vulnerability sell blockbuster action films.

Yet women are in the strange and unique position of also being spectators, consumers of their very own image, their very own objectification. At the same time that we witness our own representation, we are also, so often, denied a place in that process of representation—denied a voice—so that more often than not those images of ourselves that stare at us from the glossy pages of the women's magazines or from the glowing eye of the television screen are not of our own creation. They are, in more senses than one, truly "man-made." Teresa de Lauretis asserts that "as [a] historical individual, the female viewer is also positioned in the films of classical cinema as spectator-subject; she is thus doubly bound to the very representation which calls on her directly, engages her desire, elicits her pleasure, frames her identification, and makes her complicit in the production of (her) woman-ness."[37]

It is no accident that the feminist project has been deeply concerned from its inception with "the cultural"; even the founding texts of the "second wave" of feminism (Betty Friedan on women's magazines, Kate Millet and Simone de Beauvoir on fiction) delved into the ways in which the everyday objects of cultural consumption are as much a part of the maintenance of patriarchal social relations as are the inequities of a sexist workplace. Annette Kuhn notes, "One of the major theoretical contributions of the women's movement has been its insistence on the significance of cultural factors, in particular in the form of socially dominant representations of women and the ideological character of such representations, both in constituting the category 'woman' and in delimiting and defining what has been called the 'sex/gender' system."[38] Speaking specifically about film criticism, E. Ann Kaplan points out that feminist cultural work has a long history, beginning with the first moments of the women's movement in the 1960s: "The study of images of women in film dates back to work by the National Organization for Women in the late 1960's; to the pioneering journal, *Women and Film*, published from 1970–1972; to film journals like *Jump Cut* that made feminist approaches a central part of their format; and, finally, to the emergence in

1976 of a journal, *Camera Obscura*, specifically devoted to feminist film theory."[39]

Feminist cultural criticism is a double-edged project. It is a critique of existing (patriarchal) representations as well as a construction of alternative or oppositional cultural images and practices. The line between cultural criticism and cultural practice is indeed a fine one for feminists.[40] Rosemary Betterton[41] goes so far as to propose that feminist criticism is a challenge to representation itself because of the interdisciplinary nature of feminist criticism and the ways in which the feminist movement, by positioning women as viewing subjects, has challenged both the traditional divisions between high art and mass culture and the ideologies of objectivity and neutrality. Other feminists have also argued for the unique relationship between women and popular culture, stating that "the feminist critique is a critique of culture at once from within and from without, in the same way in which women are both *in* the cinema as representation and *outside* the cinema as subjects of practices."[42]

Tania Modleski points out that notions of mass culture and notions of the feminine have historically been bound together, mass culture being seen as feminized culture and denigrated on those terms, which sets up a hierarchical opposition between femininity/consumption/reading and masculinity/production/writing.[43] Judith Williamson claims for women a position as a sort of transcendent signifier for other "differences." In a fascinating essay on the relationship between femininity and colonization as embodied in print advertisements, Williamson argues that sexual difference "carries" other differences because "woman" is seen as a "natural" category to which other differences (less easily naturalizable) can be grafted.[44] If women do have a unique position within popular culture, then feminist theories of representation might themselves occupy a privi-

leged space within the discourses on culture. We will return
to this controversial suggestion later.

This book sets out to explore this terrain of feminist cultural theory, although I do not attempt to review every theoretical move and development in this enormous field I am
calling feminist cultural studies. The goal, rather, is three-
fold: to critically introduce readers to the main concepts
and theoretical frameworks of feminist cultural criticism;
to place these concepts and frameworks in the historical
context that produced them; and, finally, to present a
model of a feminist cultural criticism that is at once intertextual, multidisciplinary, and deeply invested in the demystification of patriarchal images and the construction of
feminist ones. The examples and case studies I will use are
drawn from a variety of mainstream popular media, particularly film and television but also advertisements and
occasionally music.[45]

The intention of this book is thus *not* to provide a com-
prehensive review of these various feminist theories of representation. Rather, it is to sketch out broadly the major
concepts and themes of the field and to begin to suggest
possibilities for alternative ways of understanding the
representation of women. To oversimplify, there have been
two primary strands in feminist theorizing on representation and popular culture. These approaches have vastly
divergent social histories, one deriving largely from sociological and empirical communications research, the other
cohering around a distinctly different set of assumptions
and preoccupations that might be called "postmarxist" or
even "poststructuralist."[46] I argue here that these two positions—although seemingly in opposition—in fact have
more in common than either would care to admit, particularly concerning their theorization of the relationship
between culture and social relations.

First, I examine what I call the "images" perspective,

where meaning is perceived as readily apparent and judged in terms of its sexist, or nonsexist, content and characterization. This position is shown to be limited both politically by its liberal assumptions and intellectually by its reflection model of cultural production and consumption. Although it has often provided useful data and stressed the necessity of empirical research, this view remains locked into an overly simplistic understanding of the uses of the mass media. This approach has largely been superseded by the critical tools of semiotics, structuralism, and psychoanalysis, yet it remains important both as a counterpoint to later work and in relation to the development of differing models of communications research.

I then discuss what I call the "signification" perspective, which posits itself overtly as an alternative to the dominant mode of cultural inquiry. Although this position is shown to have numerous advantages over the previous one—particularly in its recognition of the interactive and necessarily unstable nature of the production of meaning—it, too, fails to adequately include social context in the close analysis of representation.

Following this critical, historical review, I examine central concepts and frameworks of feminist cultural theory, from theories of the male gaze to questions of narrative to concerns around consumption and viewing. These areas of research and theory are necessarily overlapping; I hope the reader will be tolerant when the moments of overlap slip into moments of repetition. The book continues in chapter 5 with a case study of backlash images in the 1980s and early 1990s. This chapter is intended to "model" a way of doing feminist cultural analysis that places those representations within the larger context of a historical and social moment and also relates the images to other discourses, such as the prevailing political debates.

While but a snapshot view of the backlash years, this chapter is intended to illustrate the contextual, intertextual framework I endorse.

Finally, I look briefly at the work of the Centre for Contemporary Cultural Studies in Birmingham, England, as expressing an affinity with feminist critique in its insistence on an interactional and experiential definition of culture. Although this model should not be adopted wholesale, it does offer interesting possibilities for the development of feminist cultural studies. This third alternative entails an engagement with "material girls" in the context of a theory that *starts* from a feminist standpoint and proceeds with its intellectual borrowings with care and caution.

Throughout, I am concerned with elaborating the specificity of feminist cultural criticism, both in relation to social theory in general and in relation to the mass media at large. To a great extent, this is a question of methodology (for example, what makes a cultural theory "feminist"), a question that continues to plague feminist theorists eager to construct new methodologies and deeply wary of the risks of "borrowing" from other theoretical frameworks. It is also a question of the relationship of women to images and to the process of representation in general: Do women have a *particular* relationship to cultural imagery, as has been suggested by theorists like Williamson and Betterton? How are we to understand the relationship between the representation of woman and women's actual lived experience? These questions will in no way be fully answered in this book; rather, they will serve as a type of litmus test to gauge the usefulness of particular feminist analyses. It is on this last question, in particular, that feminist theories of representation will either stand or fall.

It is my contention that, while there is assuredly no one

way of doing good feminist cultural work, there are ways that tie in to different kinds of social and political insights and practices. The kind of intertextual, sociological, and contextual analysis I propose explicitly and implicitly asks deeply social questions of cultural objects and cultural processes. This book provides a critique of the narrowly textual and overly psychoanalytic focus of much recent feminist culture criticism and tries to move us in the direction of an intertextual, contextual, materialist feminism.

1

From Images of Women to Woman as Image

Adjusting the Set

It is vital to recognize that early feminist cultural criticism developed alongside the "second wave" of American feminism in the later 1960s and into the 1970s. It must be understood therefore in conjunction with the wider history of early feminist politics. Not coincidentally, the burgeoning of sex-role research in the mass media that began to appear in the pages of academic journals arrived simultaneously with the explosion of the women's movement onto the social and cultural scene. Annette Kuhn sees 1972 as the watershed year for feminist film theory in particular: "In North America, a number of women's film festivals—the first New York International Festival of Women's Films (1972) and the Toronto Women and Film Festival (1973)—coincided with the publication of three books of feminist film criticism: Molly Haskell's *From Reverence to Rape* (1975), Marjorie Rosen's *Popcorn Venus* (1973) and

Joan Mellen's *Women and Their Sexuality in the New Film* (1974)."[1]

Central to these early years of feminism was what might be described as the consciousness-raising impulse: the need and desire to "tell all" about women's situation, to expose the blatant and exploitative sexism of a male dominant society, to *describe* patriarchy. Naturally, a central part of this description of patriarchy had to do with exposing the myriad ways in which our culture perpetuated and reproduced sexist and male-dominant understandings of women and women's lives. Literature, art, film, advertisements, and, more obviously, pornography, were subjected to feminist intellectual and political attack. As with any marginal movement struggling to find a place for itself, the women's movement was confronted with either the apathy or the outright ridicule of the mainstream media. The growing self-consciousness of the women's movement about the power of the media in portraying the feminist struggle led to an awareness of the need to analyze the media from a feminist perspective. Indeed, significant studies such as Gaye Tuchman's essay in *Hearth and Home* on the treatment of the women's movement in the newspapers dealt explicitly with the role of the media in the denigration of the movement.[2]

The feminist awareness of the importance of the media in defining the terrain on which the struggle was to be waged also led to a number of encounters with the media by feminist groups eager to have some visible role in mapping that terrain. Feminist political activism, from its earliest days, often targeted systems of representation as the most visible and most blatant perpetrators of the objectification and denigration of women and the women's movement. The activity surrounding the Miss America contest in September 1968 was a classic example of feminists using the media—capitalizing on an already established media event—to protest the representation of women in general, typified by the cattle-auction objectification of women in beauty contests. The "No More Miss America!" document of August 1968 suggested the dual aim of both protesting the dominant images of women and exhibiting alternative images of liberated women embodied in the feminist protestors: "On September 7th in Atlantic City, the Annual Miss America Pageant will again crown 'your ideal.' But this year, reality will liberate the contest auction-block in the guise of 'genyooine' de-plasticized, breathing women. . . . We will protest the image of Miss America, an image that oppresses women in every area in which it purports to represent."[3]

In more recent years, attacks by feminists on systems of representation have centered on pornography, from the picketing of record stores that display album covers depicting abused women to the firebombing of porn stores and movie theaters. In a more liberal vein, feminists have consistently argued for "better" representation of women in all media forms and have successfully exerted pressure on media professionals and government officials to implement changes and to initiate studies and research.

Thus, early feminist criticism grew out of, or was at the very least connected to, feminist politics and interventions. Clearly, radical feminist politics, typified by the Miss America action, were not directly informed by social science research into the images of women in quite the same way as were government studies like *Window Dressing on the Set*.[4] But this feminist activism did provide a context for the research that began to emerge. Often discussed under the general heading of "sex-role research in the mass media," this research work had its origins in early feminist critique (writings by Betty Friedan and Kate Millet, for example) as well as in more mundane, sociologically

oriented communications research. That early feminist
researchers turned first to content analysis is no accident.
In attempting to expose the existence of male dominance
to an audience used to ideologies of equality and "equal
representation," early researchers turned to a methodology both readily available and helpful in detailing the per-
vasiveness of stereotypical imagery. Taking as their object
of analysis the images of women in the mass media, researchers explored sexism and sex-role stereotyping in a
wide variety of media forms, including television, film,
comic books, and newspapers. This exploration of sex roles
and stereotypes was thus generally concerned with documenting the existence of sexism in the mass media, either
through the study of "effects" of sexism in the media on
audiences (particularly children) or through content analyses "designed to measure certain aspects of a media message (e.g. how many male to female characters; what types
of behavior patterns do female characters exhibit as com-
pared with male characters)."[5]

The "images" perspective of much early feminist communications research therefore differed little from the
dominant paradigms of communications research prevailing at the time. The theoretical assumptions behind this
work assumed an understanding of the media as: (1) a
reflection of dominant social values, that is, media images
as the symbolic manifestation of prevailing social norms
and ideals; and (2) a primary, or even the primary, social-
izing agent for all Americans, but most particularly with
children, that is, the mass media as a teacher, a transmitter of messages and meanings. Methodologically, the
commitment was firmly to quantitatively based content
analyses and effects studies, themselves embedded within
the tradition of American positivist sociology. Thus studies within this "images" perspective regale us with facts

and figures on the portrayal of women in the mass media.

With 1990s feminist hindsight, the results of these studies seem fairly obvious. In her 1975 article on sex-role research in the mass media, Linda Busby reviewed the findings to date within content analyses and effects studies. Her thorough review included work done on daytime and prime-time television, television commercials, magazine advertisements and fiction, and children's programming.[6] The findings were as one would expect: stereotypical and traditional images of women predominate in all media forms, although a few studies did indicate a higher percentage of strong female characters on daytime television. The findings of the effects studies were correspondingly bleak:

- Media users personalize media content and thereby become directly involved in it.
- Sex of the media user is an important factor in the user's utilization and recall of the media content.
- Youngsters use media to gain insight into roles they will fill in later life.
- Youngsters model behavior they see in the media.[7]

These early studies described the persistence of sexist imagery and the relegation of women (who are consistently underrepresented) to a limited set of roles largely defined within the world of the family and the home. Busby concluded that the content analyses showed that "sex roles in the mass media are traditional and do not yet reflect the impact of the recent women's movement."[8] Another researcher argued that these limited and stereotyped roles were at odds with the changing reality of American society and, in fact, were "preparing youngsters for a world that no longer exists."[9]

This last point is important, for much of this early

work—tied as it was to the women's movement—was concerned with the impact of the movement (and the impact of the real social changes fostered by that movement) on the images of women in the mass media. Feminist researchers often attempted to track the relationship between this new social movement and the mass media: Were new, "positive" images being created? Was there a backlash against the women's movement? Did the media reflect the new demographics and include working women in its repertoire of socially acceptable portrayals? Was the movement itself being systematically ignored by the mainstream press and news agencies?

Gaye Tuchman, in her much referenced 1976 essay "The Symbolic Annihilation of Women by the Mass Media," presented the verdict on these questions as painfully clear. Reviewing the research in the field, Tuchman concluded that the mass media maintained sex-role stereotyping even in the face of a changing social reality in which women were increasingly active in the work force and were beginning to define themselves not only as wives and mothers but also as workers. Tuchman analyzed this in terms of a "culture lag" between the mass media's portrayal of women and the reality of life for women in contemporary society. In other words, while Tuchman maintained a reflection hypothesis, she also claimed that "the mass media deal in symbols and their symbolic representations may not be up-to-date. A time lag may be operating, for nonmaterial conditions, which shape symbols, change more slowly than do material conditions. This notion of a time lag (or a 'culture lag,' as sociologists term it) may be incorporated into the reflection hypothesis."[10]

George Gerbner, in his essay "The Dynamics of Cultural Resistance" in *Hearth and Home*, claimed that things were getting *worse* for women in the mass media, in large part due to a backlash against the women's movement. For Gerbner, as for Tuchman, women are "symbolically annihilated" in the mass media through a variety of strategies used to diffuse the impact of the women's movement and render it neutral and trivial.[11] Gerbner's Cultural Indicators project at the Annenberg School at the University of Pennsylvania—the first full-scale television study that used both content analysis and effects or cultivation analysis, and which continues to this day—often provided the data for the studies of images of women that were done by feminist communications researchers in the early 1970s. His general, early conclusion—that male images greatly outnumber female images in the media and that the television world portrays both women and nonwhites as victims—is quite often the accepted starting point for more detailed feminist analyses.

So, on the one hand, the early feminist media researchers had an almost conspiratorial notion of the mass media: their view was that women were being actively "annihilated" within representation. On the other hand, although this conspiratorial tone often cropped up, more important still is that feminist communications researchers generally assumed an understanding of the media as a primary *transmitter* of our social and cultural heritage.

In *Hearth and Home*, Tuchman summed up this somewhat contradictory approach, which stressed both the reflection model and the socialization model:

> The mass media perform two tasks at once. First, with some culture lag, they reflect the dominant values and attitudes in society. Second, they act as agents of socialization, teaching youngsters in particular how to behave. Watching lots of television leads children and adolescents to believe in traditional sex roles: Boys should work, girls should not. The same sex-role stereotypes are found in the

media designed especially for women. They teach that women should direct their hearts toward hearth and home.[12]

Both Tuchman and Gerbner thus at least attempted to study the portrayals of women in the emerging social context of feminism. Although their methods and findings were highly problematic, their concern with giving the women's movement a "fair shake" in the mass media was genuine and valuable. Most of the research, however, remains at the quantitative and descriptive level.

When theorists of this sort do venture beyond the head-counting, descriptive level, their remedies are often *prescriptive*, urging television executives and government officials alike to institute policy changes that put more women in the media business and portray them in more "accurate" and less stereotyped ways. This prescriptiveness is oriented toward members of the professional/managerial class, who are urged, in the name of "science" (the statistics) to respond to the demands of the researchers for "better" images. The prescriptive focus assumes an understanding of the media as the all-powerful "gatekeepers" of public opinion, and further identifies these gatekeepers predominantly as white men. In keeping with this emphasis on the gatekeeping role of media professionals, there has also been an examination of the relationship between the male hegemony of the "consciousness industries" and the sexist content of the images produced, thus making an argument not only for more "positive" images, but also for more women media producers: "It is probably true to say that this view represented a widespread and 'commonsense' position in the women's movement from its beginning. The connections between sexist stereotyping and women's subordination seemed self-evident. Remove or change offending imagery in the media and, it was argued, women could be shown *as they really are*."[13]

Most of this early research, oriented as it was toward traditional social science–based mass communications studies, focused largely on advertisements, magazines, television, and newspapers. Film studies, attached to a more humanistic tradition, received much less attention. Molly Haskell's 1973 study of women in film, *From Reverence to Rape*, and Marjorie Rosen's *Popcorn Venus*, published in the same year, were the rare exceptions, yet they do not accurately fall into this sociological mode, though they are often associated with it. Haskell and Rosen *were* concerned with stereotypes, yet their approach was historical and rather anecdotal, attempting to weave "social context" in with an analysis of women's roles in film. They made use of the feminist understandings of sex roles and stereotypes, but in a way that was qualitatively, rather than quantitatively, based.

As a whole, early feminist researchers worked largely within the dominant framework of a quantitative, content-based methodology, focusing on the enumeration of stereotypical images and the overall dominance of men in the media images themselves as well as in the media industry. In this sense, then, early feminist research can be seen as a classic case of the "woman question" being applied to a preexisting framework of analysis.

It is easy to reject this early research out of hand and to criticize it for its theoretical simplicity and adherence to dominant research traditions. To its credit, however, this early "images of women" work was often used directly in the service of consciousness raising and pressure-group politics, or more indirectly in the radical feminist encounters with the media, such as the Miss America action. Feminist communications researchers contributed to the process of consciousness raising by documenting sexism and male dominance where previously these constructs had been ignored or taken for granted. For students of the media, this initial step was vital, for it opened up the possibility of critically analyzing and challenging women's exclusion, invisibility, silence, and objectification. For example, studies by the newly formed National Organization for Women helped to point out the prevalence of stereotypes and sexist imagery in the context of a broader campaign for increased political awareness of sexism. Thus, "while these studies suffer from an underdeveloped theoretical framework, they clearly stress the liberal idea of increasing women's public visibility and criticize traditional stereotypes."[14]

In addition, it is essential to remember that studies such as Tuchman's and Haskell's, flawed as they were, helped pave the way for the flourishing of feminist cultural criticism that we witness today. In opening up this new ground, these researchers often paid more attention to the historical and social context in which media images were produced than do the more "qualitative" researchers of today (a point we shall return to later). In sum, the worth of this early work should not be underestimated: "It is important to recognize the value of such studies, both as a point of departure for students first encountering the subject and for historians and sociologists who seek more detailed information about the relation of stereotypical images to the epochs that produced them."[15]

Signifying "Woman"

The critiques of the "images of women" approach have been many and have taken a number of different forms, both feminist and nonfeminist. In this section I briefly review the central points of criticism that undergird this larger shift from "images of women" to "woman as image." Let me stress that this shift is by no means a simple and chronological one. In fact, it is perhaps more accurate to see these different perspectives In an international context, for the countries across the Atlantic were the first to champion feminist uses of semiotics, structuralism, and psychoanalysis in cultural critique. The reasons for this development abroad are in some sense obvious. The stubborn dominance of positivism and quantitative methodology in American social science has been well charted by critical theorists. Early studies of the mass media found their home in the social sciences and thus developed alongside and within the dominant paradigms of mainstream social science. Conversely, on the continent, and to a lesser extent in Great Britain, cultural criticism was linked to a humanities tradition and therefore more influenced by intellectual traditions and "high theory" than the rigidly quantitative and somewhat antitheoretical position of American social science. In any case, British feminists such as Laura Mulvey and Claire Johnston were among the first to appropriate the "new" cultural paradigms for feminism, roughly around the same time (middle 1970s) that American feminists were developing the critique of sex roles and stereotypes outlined in the previous section. So, although the positions were in some ways synchronic, the work discussed in this section certainly did present itself (at least initially) as a polemic against the "images of women" literature. In addition, while "images of women" research continues to be done in a variety of academic and political locations, it has been largely discredited by progressive cultural analysts, or those working within a critical tradition of media studies.

Probably the major criticism of this "images of women"

model centers around its conceptualization of the mass media and the process of making meaning. As was pointed out previously, early feminist communications research often relied on a reflection model of culture; the media reflect "reality" like a mirror, exemplified in the term *image*: "The very concept 'image' assumes the media can somehow directly reflect 'reality' rather as if they were a mirror on the world. This view of the media inevitably leads to dismay and affront if the media 'falsify,' 'omit' and 'distort'—i.e. create 'unrealistic' images of women (King and Stott, 1977; (Ed.) Tuchman, 1978; Friedan, 1963; Epstein, 1978; Weibel, 1977 and others)."[16] The assumption is that there exists, somewhere in the world, a "real" woman who can be revealed to us through imagery, if only the false, negative, inaccurate, untrue imagery is stripped away: "The term implies a juxtaposition of two separable elements— women as a gender or social group versus representations of women, or a real entity, women, opposed to falsified, distorted or male views of women. It is a common misconception to see images as merely a reflection, good or bad, and compare 'bad' images of women (glossy magazine photographs, fashion advertisements, etc) to 'good' images of women ('realist' photographs of women working, housewives, older women, etc)."[17] Media images are seen as having a direct and unmediated relationship with the "reality" they either distort or reflect. The mirror that media hold up to the world can be either undistorted and clear or fractured and fuzzy, but it is a mirror nonetheless. In this approach, the media are seen to reflect a sexist society and/ or the interests of male media professionals: "The frame of reference for all this work is defined by a shared and usually implicit assumption concerning the relationship between cinematic representation and the 'real world': that a film, in recording or reflecting the world in a direct or mediated fashion, is in some sense a vehicle for transmitting meanings which originate outside of itself—within the intentions of film makers, perhaps, or within social structures."[18]

The flip side of this reflection model is a view of the media derived from theories of sex roles and socialization. If the reflection model posits the media as a mirror to social "reality," the socialization model argues that the media teach us sex-stereotyped roles and behaviors. Although there is, of course, a certain commonsense truth to both these assertions (the media do have some relation to the social world, the media do teach us some things in some ways), meaning is still seen as being read from the images themselves in a direct, coherent, and uncontradictory way. The socialization hypothesis (in its most stark and simplified form, often called the "hypodermic model") assumes a one-way flow between image and viewer, with the image acting on the viewer by prescribing roles and behaviors to a largely unspecified and undifferentiated receiver of the cultural message. In other words, there is no sense of the role of the spectator in constructing meaning; an image simply "means" something (determined by its characterization and content), which then is unproblematically received by the viewer. As Rosemary Betterton summarizes this problem, "Recourse to the concept of socialization alone . . . can only provide a partial explanation. It cannot fully explain the different ways in which certain images affect us . . . nor on what basis we might make critical distinctions between different images. It also does not explain why women might respond to the same image in different ways."[19] For example, understanding Madonna as a stereotype of the sexually objectified woman gives us little insight into the complex reactions of the young girls who idolize her as a signifier of their own nascent sexuality.

Along with reflection and socialization, the third fundamental ingredient of the "images" perspective concerns stereotypes. Central to the early critique of images of women was a description of the stereotypical representations of women and how these stereotypes limited women's options and possibilities in the "real world." While it has been much easier to criticize the reflection and socialization models for their simplistic understanding of how meaning is produced, the question of stereotypes remains more difficult. Many theorists in recent years have attempted to reclaim the idea of stereotypes for a more critical feminist analysis, yet this issue continues to be a point of contention among feminist analysts of culture.[20]

The focus in early feminist work on stereotypes, though important, failed fundamentally to address the social origin of this phenomenon and thus ignored the most interesting analytical aspect: how is it that stereotypes have meaning for us? Stereotypes work only because they must, in some way, speak to perceived "real" attributes or qualities. Stereotypes often enlarge on or even parody aspects of personality or group identity that have assumed a certain "commonsense" veracity. The ideological effectiveness of stereotypes is based on the experience of them as not simply "erroneous" or "false," but rather as structurally reinforced ideological forms of repression.[21] Thus, while there are certainly some stereotypes that are simply created out of whole cloth (for example, blondes have more fun and/or are "ditsy"), the majority of stereotypes emerge from a naturalizing of selective traits of certain groups. For example, the stereotype that women are more relational and emotionally sensitive than are men is based on no small amount of experiential reality. That observation becomes a stereotype, however, when it is taken to be both natural and innate in women, and when it is generalized

to the entire female population. In addition, most stereotypes are not neutral; they are deeply embedded in structures of oppression and domination and become prescriptions for behavior and modes of social control. So the
stereotype of women as more emotional has vast social and
political implications and reverberations, such as the use
of that stereotype as justification for certain forms of job
discrimination.

Although stereotypes certainly exist in the mass media,
it is important to ask more complex questions about how,
exactly, we come to recognize certain images and representations *as stereotypes*. Does the identification of a
stereotype by a critic help us to understand how that image
is "read" by spectators? Who is to say what is a stereotype
and what is a more "realistic" portrayal? For some viewers, the character Roseanne in the hit sitcom of the same
name is anything but a stereotype (Figure 4). Many fans
see her as a working-class heroine, a tough, witty woman
who refuses to conform to male standards of beauty and
who remains proudly sexual as well. For others, she is more
like Ralph Kramden in drag, reinforcing the stereotype that
working-class families are fat, lazy, dirty, and careless in
their child-rearing practices. On the other hand, the show
has been touted as a more "realistic" image of family life
that gives the lie to the stereotypical *Father Knows Best*
domestic bliss scenarios. It is thus difficult to identify
stereotypes, particularly if one sees meaning as being produced in a relational context. Sex-role stereotypes have
meaning and "work" only because they refer to *collective*
identities and to collective, or group, experiences of the
construction and placement of roles and identities.

In addition, stereotypes change and evolve over different historical time periods and within different cultural
contexts. So, for example, Madonna successfully used the

Figure 4.   Roseanne breaks the June Cleaver mold in her depiction
of a tough, funny, sexual working-class mother. (ABC, 1993, photo
courtesy of Photofest)

stereotype of the conniving blonde bombshell (itself
already parodied by Marilyn Monroe in the film *Gentlemen Prefer Blondes*) in her music video *Material Girls,* in
which she simultaneously employed the stereotype and
deconstructed it by showing it to be just another "performance." The use of stereotypes by "images of women"
researchers, however, tended to treat stereotypes as if they
were fixed, false impositions rather than shifting, contested, complex processes.

The focus on sex *roles* also misses an essential point
about representation—the point Ferdinand de Saussure
(the French linguist and father of semiotics) made—that
meaning is made through *difference* and thus needs to be
seen *relationally*. Quantitative content analysis might provide a good picture of women's limited roles in the media,
but these static roles cannot directly translate into an

understanding of women's actual lives. In other words, the static concept of roles does not allow us to understand the more flexible and relational positionings created by mass media images, or the ways in which women's different "roles" often come into conflict and contradiction with each other. In addition, the term *roles* seems to imply a voluntaristic account of social identity: we all play roles, we can all play different roles if we so choose. This view avoids a deeper analysis of the gendered relations of power involved in the construction of gender identity.

We now confront the key problem in the "images of women" approach. For if meaning is seen as readily available to the cultural consumer and to the cultural critic (for example, woman in kitchen means housewife means stereotype means negative image), then the process of changing representation becomes one of "adjusting" images so that they provide a less stereotyped and more "positive" and more "real" version of women's lives. The problems with this model should be obvious. In the first place, who is to say what is more "real" or "positive"? More important, this emphasis on the transparency of images ignores the social context of image production, the role of the viewer in creating meaning, and the specificity of the mass media form itself, as Annette Kuhn notes: "Precisely because of its focus on images and roles, there are a number of questions that cannot readily be addressed within the terms of reference of this approach. It tends, for instance, to take readings . . . very much at face value, and to focus criticism based on such readings upon surface features of story and character."[22]

Many feminists have also taken issue with the reformist strategy suggested by the prescriptive focus of early "image" critics, a strategy that falls into the same problems as liberal feminist politics and theory. While "more women" or "better images" might expand our cultural horizons, they will not fundamentally challenge the patriarchal "ways of seeing" embedded in the process of representation. To argue for less stereotyped images avoids an attack on the deep structures of the signifying practices that produce such images in the first place. It also sidesteps an attack on the even larger social context of patriarchy in which those image-making systems are embedded. In addition, a reformist strategy implies that by changing the images themselves one changes the reception of them—that "positive images" mean that little girls will be socialized in "better" and less sexist ways. This paradigm assumes a simple, one-way communication that ignores any role for the audience/spectator in producing meaning in an *interaction* with the image. Another strategy of the "better images" approach is to place more women in the media industries, which elides the distinction between "woman" and "feminist": will more women in the media institutions necessarily produce more *feminist* images?

The spectator is also left unanalyzed. For example, the "reading" by a single white woman in New York City of *Cagney and Lacey*, the popular police drama of the 1980s, might differ from that of a suburban housewife and mother in Iowa, and a working-class mother might experience the opulence and power of Alexis in *Dynasty* as a judgment on her life, whereas a boardroom executive might find those qualities thrilling and affirming. The widely divergent opinions of Madonna among feminists, who alternately condemn her as a negative and sexualized role model for young girls and celebrate her as a powerful and self-directed symbol of active female desire, should point to the limitations of an analysis that rigidly defines images by a previously constructed code of stereotypes. All this is by way of exposing the problems inherent in a model of socialization that assumes a direct and unproblematic relationship between images and how people behave and what they actually think. As later theorists have argued, the relationship between images and everyday life, between culture and society, is hardly so simple and unmediated.

Central to this new "signification" paradigm, then, was an invigorated concern with the productiveness of images. If images of women were no longer to be seen as simple reflections (or misreflections) of "real" women, then feminists had to develop an analysis that stressed how representations *construct* sexual difference, rather than simply reflect it, arguing that "representation is *not* reflection but rather an active process of selecting and presenting, of structuring and shaping, of making things *mean*."[23] In other words, we began to examine how our cultural images produce this category "woman" and thus help to produce gender distinctions and gender dominance. Although there are similarities here with the socialization work of earlier years, this emphasis on the constructiveness of images is quite different in that it focuses—particularly in feminist film theory—on the specific "signifying practice" of a medium itself. For example, what is it about the history of film and film as a visual medium that so often dichotomizes women into virginal heroines or sexualized whores? How does the domestic location of television help to determine the kinds of images of women produced there? The question becomes not so much *what* sexist images are produced, but *how* they are produced and come to have meaning for us. One might ask not just "what" the icon of Madonna means for young girls, but "how" young girls come to know Madonna as an icon. How is that different from the process gone through by her gay male fans?

One can broadly characterize this development as a shift

from an "images of women" approach to a critical practice that stresses the constructedness of woman as image
or woman as sign. The debt to semiotics is obvious, as a
new emphasis is put on popular culture as a complex sign-
system that can be analyzed in terms of repeatable and
recognizable codes: "The title 'Images of Women' needs to
be challenged and replaced by the notion of woman as a
signifier in an ideological discourse in which one can identify the meanings that are attached to woman in different
images and how the meanings are constructed in relation
to other signifiers in that discourse."[24] The (new) claim is,
therefore, that the entire cultural notion of "woman" is
itself constructed in and through images rather than
somehow "residing" in the images themselves— "woman"
is constructed as "a set of meanings which then enter cultural and economic circulation on their own account."[25]
Whereas in the previous paradigm of feminist cultural criticism, "woman" herself was taken to be unproblematic, this
new approach argues that the representation of women
in a patriarchal culture entails a split between real, social
women and woman *as* image constructed for male desire,
woman as sexual spectacle. In other words, feminist theorists now are claiming that it is difficult, and perhaps
impossible, to represent *women* (here meaning actual,
embodied women) within patriarchy, and that we instead
have to reckon with that which *is* represented: woman as
sign, as image, as spectacle. Feminist film theorist Teresa
de Lauretis sums up the two approaches:

> The accounts of feminist film culture produced in the mid
> to late 1970s tended to emphasize a dichotomy between
> two concerns of the women's movement and two types of
> film work that seemed to be at odds with each other: one
> called for immediate documentation for purposes of polit-
> ical activism, consciousness-raising, self-expression or the

search for "positive images" of women; the other insisted on rigorous, formal work on the medium—or better, the cinematic apparatus, understood as a social technology—in order to analyse and disengage the ideological codes embedded in representation.[26]

These two approaches appear quite distinct, and in many ways they are. Nevertheless, in the final chapter I will propose that they share some of the same problems, particularly regarding the question of the relationship between woman as image or sign and women as real, embodied, social beings. This woman/women distinction has proved central to the feminist analysis of culture but remains a difficult and problematic construct, as will be discussed in later chapters.

2

Visual Pressures
On Gender and Looking

"You've Got the Look": The Male Gaze

Much of the recent work in feminist cultural analysis has arisen around issues concerning the relationship between gender and looking. Since "looking" or "sight" is obviously such an important part of the reception of an image, it makes sense to examine the ways in which looking at images is constructed by gendered divisions and the social relations of patriarchal power. This approach is connected to the new concern with how the representations of women function; if it is true that women are so often represented as sexual spectacle, as "on display" for men (which much of the early feminist critique demonstrated), then how does that "work," what are the processes that produce woman as sexual spectacle? In response to this inquiry, feminist cultural criticism has tended to move beyond the question of the sexist context of images and toward an examination of "the mechanisms of viewing."[1]

One of the first theorists to address directly the complex question of looking and its relation to gender was the marxist cultural critic John Berger, who wrote the book and television series titled *Ways of Seeing*. For Berger, patriarchal society entails that a woman be constructed as an object for the "look" of the male spectator, or the male voyeur. Berger focused on how, in our patriarchal culture with its imbalance between male and female power, women are positioned as the passive object of the male look and come to internalize this look:

> She has to survey everything she is and everything she does because how she appears to others, and ultimately how she appears to men, is of crucial importance for what is normally thought of as the success of her life. . . . *men act* and *women appear.* Men look at women. Women watch themselves being looked at. This determines not only most relations between men and women but also the relation of women to themselves. The surveyor of woman in herself is male: the surveyed female. Thus she turns herself into an object of vision: a sight.[2]

Berger argued that looking—which might be considered a relatively neutral activity—actually carries with it relations of power, access, and control. This power is precisely what determines the "difference" of women: "Women are depicted in a quite different way from men—not because the feminine is different from the masculine—but because the 'ideal' spectator is always assumed to be male and the image of woman is designed to flatter him."[3]

Ways of Seeing remains an important text for feminist cultural theorists, even though its framework is rooted in the work of the marxist cultural theorist and literary critic Walter Benjamin, and is by no means explicitly feminist in its aims. Rather, its uniqueness lies in its creative and determined efforts to break down the categories of

"high art" and "mass culture" and to show how these clas-
sifications and ways of seeing are themselves highly ideological and mystifying.

Berger examined "high art" for its construction of a gendered (and classed) way of seeing, as well as popular advertising. His focus on the classic nude as a precursor to more
apparent forms of female objectification found in modern
advertising was helpful in pushing cultural criticism to see
male power in all kinds of representations, even those considered "high art" and therefore sacrosanct. Berger pointed
out that the depiction of the nude female body in classical painting spoke a great deal about sexual politics: "Her
body is arranged in the way it is to display it to the man
looking at the picture. This picture is made to appeal to
his sexuality. It has nothing to do with her sexuality."[4] It
is also significant that Berger stressed that this process of
objectification and masculine control of the image not only
reinforced male "property" rights over women, but also
produced a female identity that internalized this view of
woman as object of male desire, so a woman "comes to
consider the *surveyor* and the *surveyed* within her as the
two constituent yet always distinct elements of her identity as a woman."[5]

In introducing the concept of gendered "ways of seeing"—and in developing a historical argument that showed
how the female body has been objectified throughout the
years—Berger paved the way both for feminist theories of
"the gaze" and for the marxist rethinking of popular culture and ideology.

This idea of the male as bearer of the look, as occupy-
ing a privileged space in the process of constructing "ways
of seeing," has been taken up by feminists of several different intellectual persuasions. Perhaps the most significant, though, is the psychoanalytic inflection offered by

Laura Mulvey in her important article for *Screen* in 1975, "Visual Pleasure and Narrative Cinema." If Berger convincingly argued that woman has been placed on the passive side of a gendered division of looking, Mulvey raised the theoretical stakes by asking the crucial question of why this is so; what is it about representation in our culture that insists on this active/passive distinction and that perpetuates the dominance of the "male gaze"? Mulvey turned to psychoanalysis, specifically Lacanian psychoanalysis, to provide a complex answer that locates the male gaze both in the particular processes of classic narrative cinema and in the psychological phenomena of scopophilia, voyeurism, and fetishism. As Mary Ann Doane notes, Mulvey's work was decisive:

> A theory of the unconscious was perceived as absolutely crucial to the comprehension of the cinema as the realm of fantasy and desire and the activator of mechanisms of voyeurism and fetishism. Laura Mulvey's "Visual Pleasure and Narrative Cinema" (1975) provided a paradigm which every feminist film critic henceforth felt obliged to confront precisely because it seemed to demonstrate the "perfect fit" between the concepts and scenarios of psychoanalysis—the Oedipus complex, scopophilia, castration, fetishism, identification—and the cinematic imaging and narrativization of sexual difference.[6]

It is hard to overestimate how central this concept has been for feminist cultural studies. It introduced the issue of male power into the most intimate aspect of the representational process: sight. It moved beyond the notion of stereotypes and claimed that the objectification of women was not an "added on" attraction, but rather endemic to the very structure of image making. Kaja Silverman, writing in the classic collection *Re-Vision: Essays in Feminist Film Criticism,* clearly states the significance of the concept of the gaze: "It is by now axiomatic that the female subject is the object rather than the subject of the gaze in mainstream narrative cinema. She is excluded from authoritative vision not only at the level of the enunciation, but at that of the fiction. At the same time she functions as an organizing spectacle, as the lack which structures the symbolic order and sustains the relay of male glances."[7]

Mulvey and others have asserted that there are two main pleasures of looking in Hollywood film: voyeurism and fetishism. The voyeur experiences pleasure in seeing without being seen, which is associated with power and control over the image. The eye of the camera is like an eye looking through a peephole: "Voyeurism is a way of taking sexual pleasure by looking at rather than being close to a particular object of desire, like a Peeping Tom. And Peeping Toms can always stay in control. Whatever may be going on, the Peeping Tom can always determine his own meanings for what he sees."[8] Classic examples of this scenario would be Tony Perkins looking through the hole in the wall at an undressing Janet Leigh in *Psycho,* and the scene in David Lynch's *Blue Velvet* in which a young man watches, through the slats of a closet door, a woman being raped (Figure 5).

The fetishistic look has to do with the endowment of some object or body part with sexual meaning. Mulvey relied strongly on Freud's essay on fetishism, suggesting that the erotic image of a woman can trigger the memory of the childhood process whereby the boy observes that the mother does not have a penis, thus producing a sense of horror. The fetishism derives from the disavowal and denial of that "castration"—as Gaylyn Studlar puts it, the boy/man turns an object into a "symbolic replacement of the mother's missing penis."[9] In film, this often takes the form of a sexualization of women's bodies or part of their

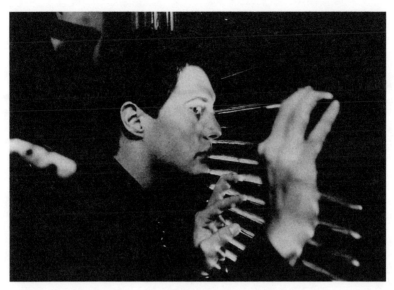

Figure 5.   An innocent young man takes a furtive peek at the sexual escapades of a subjugated woman in David Lynch's *Blue Velvet*. (De Laurentiis Entertainment Group, 1986; photo courtesy of Museum of Modern Art Film Stills Archive)

bodies, ascribing a phallic connotation to a female body part (legs, breasts) in order to recuperate the woman and rid himself of the threat of otherness generally, and the threat of castration specifically: "Woman as representation signifies castration, inducing voyeuristic or fetishistic mechanisms to circumvent her threat."[10]

This fetishistic look is also clearly part of the representation of women in advertising, to the point where a woman is represented only as a body part: "In ads women are frequently represented in a 'fragmented' way. . . . Women are signified by their lips, legs, hair, eyes or hands, which stand, metonymically—the it for the whole—for, in this case, the 'sexual' woman. Men, on the other hand, are less often 'dismembered.'"[11] Indeed, the theory of the

male gaze seems to hold particularly well for advertisements, in which women's bodies are often fragmented,
shown as discrete body parts that are meant to represent
the whole woman. Women are urged to think of their bodies as "things" that need to be molded, shaped, and remade
into a male conception of female perfection. The frag-
mentation of the female body into parts that should be
"improved" or "worked on" often results in women having a self-hating relationship with their bodies. Such frag-
mentation is closely related to the marketplace and
consumerism, thus linking up the powers of looking with
the powers of ownership and consumption: "It is the multiplication of areas of the body accessible to marketing.
Here, areas not previously seen as sexual have become sexualized. And being sexualized, they come under the
scrutiny of the ideal. New areas constructed as sensitive
and sexual, capable of stimulation and excitement, capable of attracting attention, are new areas requiring *work*
and *products*."[12]

The darkened room of the movie theater sets into motion
a set of psychic responses that encourage both a voyeuris-
tic/scopophilic attitude and an ego identification with the
characters on the screen. Mulvey argues that woman is created as a spectacle for male desire through the gaze of the
camera (seen here as a phallic substitute), the gaze of the
men within the narrative, and the gaze of the male spectator, governed by his fear of castration and subsequent
fetishization of the female body. This position is summa-
rized by Teresa de Lauretis: "The woman is framed by the
look of the camera as icon, or object of the gaze: an image
made to be looked at by the spectator, whose look is
relayed by the look of the male character(s). The latter not
only controls the events and narrative action but is 'the
bearer' of the look of the spectator."[13]

There are three "looks" that constitute the male gaze. First is the gaze within the representation itself: men gaze at women, who become objects of the gaze; second, the spectator, in turn, is made to identify with this male gaze and to objectify the woman on the screen; and third, the camera's original "gaze" comes into play in the very act of filming; the camera here can be understood as an extension of the male eye. Mary Devereaux makes an important distinction between "literal and metaphorical" usage of the concept of male gaze: "In literal terms, the gaze is male when men do the looking. Men look both as spectators and as characters within works. In figurative terms, to say that the gaze is male refers to a way of seeing which takes women as its object. In this broad sense, the gaze is male whenever it directs itself at, and takes pleasure in, women, where women function as erotic objects."[14] She notes the distinction between "the three different gazes: that of the filmmaker, the characters within the film and the spectator."[15] First, of course, is the filmmaker. Now, of course, there are female filmmakers, but, regardless of the presence of a few women here and there, proponents of the concept of the male gaze believe that the system of filmmaking is so thoroughly male-dominated and governed by male perspectives that the gaze of the filmmaker remains male even when the person looking through the viewfinder on the camera or editing the rushes is a woman. The same would hold true for other media, particularly fashion photography, where male photographers dominate the field. This issue has been hotly debated, as recent feminists have argued for a "different way of seeing" embodied in films, television shows, and other media directed and/or produced by women.

This idea of the productive gaze as male fits in with much of feminist theory, which describes a female self largely determined by male values and prescriptions. In such a framework, the female director—herself a "victim" of patriarchal socialization and subject formation—cannot help but see herself through the eyes of the hegemonic male vision. As E. Ann Kaplan notes, male looking is never a simple mirror to a purported female gaze, because it is backed up by real social power: "Men do not simply look; their gaze carries with it the power of action and of possession which is lacking in the female gaze."[16]

The second aspect of the male gaze concerns the gaze of the male characters within the film. Not only is the entire production of films constructed through male eyes (literal or otherwise), but also the characters in the films tend to treat women as sexualized objects and to control the process of looking: "It is this sense—that the image of the woman in Hollywood film is constructed through scenography, blocking, pacing and so on in order to display her for male erotic contemplation—that feminist, psychoanalytic critics invoke when they say that the gaze in Hollywood film is masculine."[17]

The third aspect of the male gaze concerns spectatorship, and this has proven to be perhaps Mulvey's most contentious point. For she not only assumes the spectator to be male, but also believes that the voyeuristic male spectator is intimately involved in helping to produce woman as object: "In a world ordered by sexual imbalance, pleasure in looking has been split between active/male and passive/female. The determining male gaze projects its phantasy on to the female figure which is styled accordingly."[18]

An important aspect of Mulvey's argument is the contention that there is no space for an authentic female gaze, because the spectator is inevitably addressed as male, and female viewers are forced to look with the male protagonist; Rosemary Betterton points out that, as a result, "woman as spectator is offered the dubious satisfaction of identification with the heterosexual masculine gaze, voyeuristic, penetrating and powerful."[19] Doane argues that identity itself is unavailable to the female spectator, bound up as it is with the processes of voyeurism and fetishism: "The female spectator . . . in buying her ticket, must deny her sex. There are no images either *for* her or *of* her."[20]

More by implication than by explicit analysis, Mulvey addresses the problem of the female spectator in a visual world constructed for male pleasure. The male viewer may revel in his fetishistic scopophilia, getting pleasure and control from that which he sees from a distance, but the female viewer is condemned to a narcissistic pleasure, or as Betterton describes it, a "pleasure in closeness, in reflection and in identification with an image."[21] In other words, the female gaze (for Mulvey not so much a gaze as a passive spectating position) seems to be characterized either by narcissism or by a kind of masochistic identification with one's own objectification.

Doane further develops the psychoanalytic position that finds women's spectatorship "different" in that women cannot maintain the necessary distance needed to fetishize. While a man, it seems, is "destined to be a fetishist," woman "must find it extremely difficult, if not impossible, to assume the position of fetishist. That body which is so close continually reminds her of the castration which cannot be 'fetishized away.'"[22] In this construct, the female spectator is placed in a position of transvestism, in which she is either identifying with the women characters and placed in a passive/masochistic position or identifying with the male hero and masculinized.[23] Doane turns to the idea of "masquerade"—a performing of femininity that reveals its status as construction—to find some space for female resistance in the destabilization of the male look:

> Above and beyond a simple adoption of the masculine position in relation to the cinematic sign, the female spectator is given two options: the masochism of over-identification or the narcissism entailed in becoming one's own object of desire, in assuming the image in the most radical way. The effectivity of masquerade lies precisely in its potential to manufacture a distance from the image, to generate a problematic within which the image is manipulable, producible, and readable by the woman.[24]

But, as Doane asks, Why can't we simply reverse this gaze, appropriating the pleasure of looking for ourselves? Because the very reversal reinforces the terms of the binary opposition: "The male striptease, the gigolo—both inevitably signify the mechanism of reversal itself, constituting themselves as aberrations whose acknowledgement simply reinforces the dominant system of aligning sexual difference with a subject/object dichotomy. And an essential attribute of that dominant system is the matching of male subjectivity with the agency of the look."[25]

When men become the object of woman's gaze, the woman takes on a "masculine" role as bearer of the gaze and initiator of the action, and she nearly always loses her traditionally feminine characteristics (kindness, humaneness, motherliness).[26] She is often cold, driving, ambitious, and manipulative, just like the men; she may be sexy, like the ruthless Alexis on the television series *Dynasty*, but she loses her "maternal" qualities. Mulvey reconsiders the concept of the male gaze in relation to female spectators in her essay "Afterthoughts on 'Visual Pleasure and Narrative Cinema' . . . Inspired by *Duel in the Sun*."[27] In this later writing, Mulvey develops the idea of the "mobile" position of the female spectator, in which the female viewer adopts the "transvestite" position of the masculine hero, thus experiencing (uncomfortably) the power of that position even though she is unable to adopt it fully. We will return to this question of the spectator in chapter 4, as it has proved to be a site of controversy in recent debates.

Cracks in the Mirror? Implications and Challenges

Feminists working with the theory of the male gaze strongly indicted classic Hollywood cinema as being the primary culprit in producing images of woman as spectacle for male desire. As Noel Carroll points out, "Women are passive; men are active. Men carry the narrative action forward; women are the stuff of ocular spectacle, there to serve as the locus of the male's desire to savor them visually. Indeed, Mulvey maintains, on screen, women in Hollywood film tend to slow down the narrative or arrest the action, since action must often be frozen, for example, in order to pose female characters so as to afford the opportunity for their erotic contemplation."[28] The issue of point of view becomes crucial here, as Mulvey and others argue that the narrative structure and mise-en-scène of classic Hollywood film literally act out the male gaze: "The classic Hollywood film reinforces this message stylistically by confining the spectator to the point of view of the narrative hero."[29]

In addition, Mulvey stresses the relationship between spectacle and narrative:

> In Laura Mulvey's account of visual pleasure in film, the ideal psychic trajectory of the classical cinema involves the interweaving of spectacle and narrative. Within individual

films there are numerous effects of spectacle, the most obvious of which occur in the musical, whether in the way in
which the narrative is frequently subservient to performance, or in the overall preoccupation with theatricality
and performance. In a more general way, most classical
films create spectacles by defining objects of the look—
whether the look of the camera or of protagonists within
the film—so as to stage their quality of what Mulvey calls,
referring specifically to the female object of the look—their
"to-be-looked-at-ness."[30]

For Mulvey, many aspects of popular filmmaking contribute to the construction of the woman as sexualized
spectacle, including the kinds of camera shots (close-
ups), costuming, lighting, and make-up.

The implications of Mulvey's version of the male gaze
are dramatic: a disavowal of narrative cinema and the construction of a feminist avant-garde that destroyed narrative pleasure, a pleasure that, in her reading, was both
masochistic and reproductive of male dominance. Indeed,
Mulvey herself attempted to produce just such an avant-
garde film, *The Riddles of the Sphinx*, made with Peter
Wollen. She argued strongly that Hollywood films were
bankrupt for feminists, because "the mass of mainstream
film, and the conventions within which it has consciously
evolved, portrays a hermetically sealed world which
unwinds magically, indifferent to the presence of the audience, producing for them a sense of separation and play-
ing on their voyeuristic phantasy."[31] If the pleasure of film
was, for women, always tainted by a male gaze that controlled and objectified, then we must reject that very pleasure. This stricture, too, has evoked intense debate, both
for its absolute rejection of those films from which the vast
majority of us derive so much pleasure and for its insis-

tence on an avant-garde film practice that only earnest film students seem to enjoy.

Further debate has arisen over the extent to which the notion of the male gaze can be generalized to media other than film. Although the concept of the gaze has been applied successfully to the analysis of advertisements, which so clearly present woman as sexual spectacle, it is more difficult to translate to the medium of television. In its psychoanalytic version, the concept is so connected to signifying practices that depend on a darkened room and a relatively passive and fixed audience that it is questionable to what extent it applies to a medium such as television, where the televised image blurs with the familial surroundings, making the intensity of the directed male gaze much more problematic. Kaplan questions "how well . . . theories about the 'male gaze' apply to watching television, when usually there is no darkened room, where there is a small screen, and where viewing is interrupted by commercials, by people moving about, or by the viewer switching channels."[32]

John Ellis, among others, persuasively argues that the "gaze" is an inaccurate concept for television analysis because the viewer is *not* in the voyeuristic position of the cinema viewer; instead, television itself has the "look": "The viewer for TV is very far from being in a position of producing a totalising vision of the truth from the initial stance of curiosity. For broadcast TV, the regime of viewing is rather one of complicity with TV's own look at the passing pageant of life."[33] On the other hand, if one fully adopts the psychoanalytic viewpoint, which locates the origins of the male gaze in timeless infantile experiences, then the particular medium in which these processes are acted out should not alter the basic mechanism. This disjunction points to a problem with the psychoanalytic approach, which is unable to pay substantive attention to the differences among particular media forms (but more on that later).

The theory of the male gaze seems particularly relevant for representations that hinge so thoroughly on sexualized imagery and spectacle. The new world of music videos is perhaps such a site, for the short format and often nonnarrative style encourage the production of "spectacles," although numerous theorists have argued that MTV's pastiche of ambiguous, nonnarrative images and sounds often provides a greater variety of "gazes" than those in classical cinema: "The question of visual pleasure is more complicated. The objectification of women for the voyeuristic pleasure of male viewers characteristic of film has been replicated in music videos. But at the same time, creation of a female gaze by women artists is one of the most important trends in music video, suggesting that TV may offer women a space for a new investigation of female spectatorship."[34]

Clearly, Berger's original point about women as the "surveyed" of our culture rings true for various media forms, but the more distinctive concept of the male gaze as it has been used by psychoanalytic feminists raises problems, several of which will be discussed in the following chapters. In addition, Berger's development of the male gaze concept, as noted earlier, has a mixed intellectual heritage, being influenced by marxism, and in particular, the work of Walter Benjamin. But this theory has also been used more deliberately by the Mulvey-influenced feminist film critics, who elaborate the specific processes of scopophilia, fetishism, and voyeurism that were developed originally in a therapeutic/analytic context. Mulvey, along with the legions of feminist cultural critics who came before and after her, is deeply influenced by psychoanalysis and the belief that psychoanalytic concepts (whether strictly Freudian or Lacanian) are particularly appropriate for the analysis of representation. Thus feminist critics are faced with a dual heritage when discussing the male gaze. On the one hand, the term has been used rather generically to describe and analyze the objectification of women in popular culture—the myriad ways women are turned into objects for the pleasure of a male viewer. The theory of the male gaze has broad and commonsense sociological implications regarding the internalization of male standards of beauty and the orientation of women toward male approval and "performance" for male desire.[35]

Rosalind Coward's work on female desires and how they are constructed in a commodity culture relies heavily on (Berger-like) ideas of the "look" and male control of visual imagery. Traversing advertisements, the fashion industry, and the tabloid press, Coward stresses the inhibiting and debilitating results of male-dominant image making, which turns women into objects to be packaged and sold—to men and to themselves.[36] And feminist theorists such as Susanne Kappeler have used the "look" concept to indict representation as the cornerstone of patriarchy: "The fundamental problem at the root of men's behaviour in the world, including sexual assault, rape, wife battering, sexual harassment, keeping women in the home and in unequal opportunities and conditions, treating them as objects for conquest and protection—the root problem behind the reality of men's relations with women, is the way men see women, is seeing."[37]

However flawed by its psychoanalytic baggage and its tunnel vision in relation to spectatorship, the concept of the gaze has stressed the importance of understanding imagery as structured by the context of male dominance:

the ability to scrutinize is premised on power. This context of male dominance means that not only do men as a gender have the institutional (political and economic) power to control the actual production of culture and cultural images (that is, the heads of all major networks are male, and with few exceptions the same can be said for the film industry and advertising), but they also have the ideological power to control the form and content of the images themselves. Nevertheless, as we will see in later chapters, the reign of this concept has been seriously challenged in recent years.

3

Positioning Women
Gender, Narrative, Genre

Telling Tales

The theory of the male gaze is, as we have seen, strongly linked to a critique of classic realist narrative as inevitably producing and reproducing the diminution of women in the stories of popular culture. Thus, the textual analysis of classic Hollywood cinema became another important area for the new feminist cultural criticism. Narrative theory has a long history, both within film theory and within literary criticism. Here I focus on the specifically *feminist* appropriations of narrative analysis, without reviewing narrative theory in depth. Although narrative has been central to the analysis of culture in general, in more recent years this concern with narrative has been central to film theory and is intimately connected with the rise of structuralism within film studies, as Annette Kuhn indicates: "Work on narrative structures . . . is based on the assumption that any one narrative will share common structures with innumerable others. In other words, the presupposition of Formalist approaches to narrative analysis is that individual narratives are simply expressions of underlying structures, or ground rules, common to whole groups of narratives."[1]

Since Louis Althusser, and Lacan via Althusser, questions of narrative have been closely related to questions of subjectivity.[2] In Althusserian and post-Althusserian film theory, the subject is defined, even constructed, *as* a (fictive) subject, in and through narrative. In this structuralist sense, narrative is not simply "the story," but the vehicle through which the processes of identification and the construction of subjectivity occur. Althusser's claim, borrowing from Lacan, that ideology works by "hailing" us as subjects (what is called the process of *interpellation*), was applied to theories of narrative. In other words, we are positioned and constructed by the operations of the narrative itself, particularly by what is called the "classic realist narrative." Christine Gledhill summarizes this process: "Classic realist texts, it was argued, reproduce bourgeois ideology because they implicate the spectator in a single point of view onto a coherent, hierarchically ordered representation of the world, in which social contradictions are concealed and ultimately resolved through mechanisms of displacement and substitution. In this process, the spectator is 'interpellated' as the 'individual subject' of bourgeois ideology."[3] Feminists focusing on narrative structure are not simply concerned, therefore, with how typical plot patterns might serve to make women invisible, or to punish women, or to place women as the objects of an all-seeing, all-knowing male gaze, but with how narrative structures produce—on a deeper and perhaps unconscious level—subjectivities or identities.

The discussion of narrative not only is related to a discussion of subjectivity but also is influenced by a critique of realism itself. In this reading, the realist narrative is seen as deeply ideological, masking both the conditions of its own production and the contradictions of a patriarchal and capitalist society. Realist films, television shows, and advertisements offer themselves up as "windows on the world," thus concealing their ideological status as representations. In realism, "meaning also presents itself as 'already there' in the story, rather than as an outcome of active processes of signification. In dominant cinema, it might be said, signifiers work un-obtrusively in the service of the narrative."[4] Narrative realism, then, conveys the impression of a "point-of-view-lessness," so that it seems as if "events narrate themselves. There is no voice which tells the story, there does not appear to be a controlling consciousness that is writing the narrative for the audience."[5] Feminists have pointed out that this apparently anonymous, neutral, and nonexistent voice happens to be in a decidedly masculine register. This narrative transparency has been heavily criticized by feminist and nonfeminist film critics alike.

The concept of "suture" is central to the production of narrative realism. Theorists have argued that the actual mechanisms of the film process link the spectator with the operations of the ideology of the text. Even particular kinds of editing, shots, and staging devices are implicated in the process of making (patriarchal) meaning: "The shot/reverse shot formation is often cited as an example of cinematic suture. This involves a complex interplay of looks between camera, spectator and characters in the fiction."[6] The use of continuity editing—the attempt to project a sense of continuity in space and time—makes editing appear "invisible" so that the spectator is encouraged to read the film without effort. Continuity editing bridges time and space to create an illusion of events unfolding naturally. It is this cinematic appearance of naturalness that, so often, serves to reinforce the ideologies of "women's place" presented in films as somehow "natural," too.

If the narrative *structure* of dominant cinema utilizes certain realist conventions and implies circumscribed spectator positions, then the need to study individual audiences became a rather moot point, and close textual/structural analysis became the dominant form of film criticism. Feminist film critics, in particular, have been transformed by the "structuralisms" and have therefore redefined the "object" of their analysis, so that woman is no longer "regarded as a concrete gendered human being who happens to exist on the cinema screen rather than in 'real' life: 'she' becomes, on the contrary, a structure governing the organization of plot in a narrative or group of narratives."[7]

How does the way a story gets told help to construct certain representations of women? How do certain types of texts (particularly the classic Hollywood narrative) serve to position women in consistent and circumscribed ways? Does the narrative structure of classic Hollywood cinema, with its pattern of unity-disruption-resolution and its gendered division of looking, inevitably reinforce patriarchal ways of seeing?—these questions have been central to the feminist rethinking of the relationship between woman and narrative.

These and other issues have been addressed by psychoanalytic film theorists such as Laura Mulvey and E. Ann Kaplan, as well as by the more semiotically inclined theorist Teresa de Lauretis, in an attempt to untangle the relationship between narrative and the representation of women. In general, feminists have contended that the classic realist narrative is typically structured around a feminine enigma, and thus the woman is placed as the unknowable Other who needs to be known/resolved. The masculine agent often has the same knowledge that we, the audience, do; it is from his point of view, and rarely the woman's, that the story is oriented. Yet it is the woman who disrupts this filmic universe: "Female discourses/ female sexuality are the threats which disturb the narrative and it is these which must be contained through narrative closure."[8] De Lauretis claims that woman actually *represents* narrative closure, that the movement of the narrative toward resolution depends on the image of woman.[9] Most important, the classic narrative resolves the disrupted universe by bringing the woman back into line through some sort of punishment (death, disgrace) or through marriage and the safe enclosure of the nuclear family: "There seems . . . to be a tendency on the part of the classic Hollywood narrative to recuperate woman. Moreover, it is often woman—as a structure, character, or both—who constitutes the motivator of the narrative, the 'trouble' that sets the plot in motion."[10] But, as Kuhn has argued, the narrative is not always successful in recuperating woman, producing a narrative "excess" that can be "seen as signalling Hollywood's intermittent failure to contain woman within the confines of the classic narrative structure."[11]

Much of the feminist writing about film (and recent work on literature and television as well) has been about an attempt to discover this excess in order to "recuperate" classic cinema for feminist interpretations. Crucial to this process is the practice of "reading against the grain," where films or television shows are "read" for their absences and ruptures in an attempt to reveal the internal contradictions and produce a reading or interpretation that challenges both the dominant reading of the film and its coherency and closure. In so doing, feminists have challenged the view of classic narrative that sees it as impenetrable and completely unified and coherent. Critics have questioned the ability of the narrative to bring women "back into line," thereby continuing to challenge the "images of women" approach:

> A "reading against the grain" of the classical cinema does not assume that patriarchy is either so monolithic or so coherent as to be able to produce images that serve no other ends but its own. Theoretically then, the difference between these two approaches concerns above all different conceptions of ideology. "Images of women" suggests a relatively simple manipulative system of social control, while "reading against the grain" suggests a system full of contradictions, gaps, and slips of the tongue.[12]

There is often a disjuncture between the ideological desire to put the woman in "her place" at the end of the film and the actual structure of the narrative which sometimes contradicts that "resolution." It is in these contradictions, these excesses, that feminist film critics have often located the possibility of rereading the film so that these moments become highlighted and revealed.

One of my favorite examples of Hollywood's failure, narratively, to produce coherent and believable closure is in the classic film *Blonde Venus*, starring Marlene Dietrich (Figure 6). In this film, Dietrich (herself an enigmatic figure, thus extratextually resistant as well) plays Helen Faraday, a woman who is married to a scientist stricken ill by one of his experiments. A former singer, Helen goes back on stage to raise the money to send her husband to Switzerland for the cure he needs to survive. Remade as the Blonde Venus, she is befriended by a rich playboy (Cary Grant) who gives her the necessary money and, of course, falls in love with her. Helen sends her husband off for the cure and eventually moves in with her rich friend. When her husband returns early, he discovers her "secret" and threatens to take her young son away from her. Thus begins Helen's downward spiral, as she runs from town to town, keeping just one step ahead of the police. Eventually, thinking it best for the child, she gives up her son to the father and sinks into alcoholic degeneracy. She is transformed and turns up in Europe, a cold and "masculine"[13] star once again. The film ends with her return to New York and her reunion with husband and son, who "take her back." The nuclear family is safely reunited.

Although this summary ostensibly reads like the classic narrative of the wayward woman punished for her errant ways and finally, repentant, brought back to the domestic fold, it becomes, on closer examination, fraught with inconsistencies and confusions that make the neat closure seem artificial and silly. By looking closely at the narrative structure, we can see that, for example, Helen's initial punishment (what turns her into a bad, sexual woman that then justifies the loss of her child and then motivates the reunion) seems itself unjustified: her husband should never have left her. For Helen has become "bad" only to save her husband's life; his brutal rejection of her on his return appears unjustified and spiteful. Thus the main narrative motivation for Helen's punishment and "resurrection" is highly illogical.

In addition, in most representations of a mother losing her child she must first be shown to be a truly horrible mother; the ideology of motherhood is so strong in our culture that a mother must be depicted as deeply neglectful to merit the punishment of loss. In *Blonde Venus*, however, we have no doubt that Helen is, even in the worst of circumstances, a wonderful and loving parent. In addition, extratextual factors play into our disbelief. Dietrich was a powerful and sexual Hollywood star. The depiction of her as a chastened wife, begging to go back to her tradition-

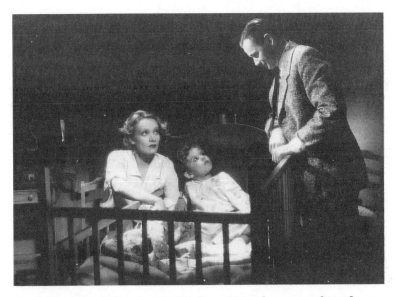

Figure 6. *Blonde Venus* stars Marlene Dietrich as everything from desperate mother on the run to glamorous star to doting, apologetic housewife—a narrative that does not quite hold together. (Paramount, 1932; photos courtesy of Museum of Modern Art Film Stills Archive)

bound husband, must have struck a false note with many viewers, particularly women who idolized Dietrich's independence and power. And the rumors of her lesbianism, which abounded in Hollywood at the time, must have seemed at odds with the depiction of a domesticated, heterosexual housewife. By film's end we experience little narrative justification for the reunion, for this reining in of a woman. Feminist film critics argue that it is precisely this narrative inconsistency that we should seek out—to elaborate and make visible the cracks in the supposedly airtight case that is male-dominant imagery.

Television critics have also focused on narrative and have stressed that the structure of the ongoing television serial, for example, needs to be seen in different narrative terms from those for classic film narrative: "The movement from event to event characteristic of cinematic narration is radically reduced in favour of the multiplication of incident, of action-clinch and of conversation. These take place in relatively self-contained segments. Segments are bound together into programmes by the repetition device of the series. This constitutes a basic ongoing problematic, which rarely receives a final resolution."[14] Because soap operas and some serials have no real resolution or closure, it is necessary to rethink the position of women in relation to this lack of closure. Is there more space for women within the structure of television serials, and if so, how does this relate to the familial environment in which one most often watches television? Martha Nochimson suggests that "by opening up narrative linearity, soap opera does not merely give a potential female subject the chance to cut a wide swath or gain spectator identification; it actually insists that she be set free."[15] Perhaps television narrative, combining a domestic environment with a relationship-based content and an ongoing, open structure allows for more space for a female viewer. As Shaun Moores points out, "Soap opera's multilevelled, open-ended narrative structures demand a viewer who is able to identify with a range of characters. Such a cultural competence is brought to the text by many women viewers as a consequence of their social placing as housewives and mothers."[16]

In sum, feminist work on narrative takes many forms. On the one hand, we need to examine how the very structure of narrative serves to reinscribe women in positions of subordination. On the other hand, we need to pay attention to the gaps in this narrative positioning of women. The scripts of popular culture are often laden with rigid patriarchal motifs, but these are not the only narratives.

Feminist studies often actively read these narratives against the grain to reveal counternarratives that offer places of possibility for the representation of women.

Nevertheless, feminist "reading against the grain" is not the whole answer to "reclaiming" mainstream representations. Judith Mayne's cautionary concern is worth quoting at length:

> A feminist reading against the grain reveals the repressed contents of classical narrative. . . . One could go on and on with examples of this sort, revealing again and again those kinds of cracks in the seams of dominant ideology. There is an undeniable if somewhat curious pleasure involved in such analysis: you can still like the classical cinema without turning it into a "bad object." But it is necessary to question the extent to which such readings as these inform the consumption of films. One of the major advantages of a reading against the grain of the classical cinema is that it allows us to analyze films from the standpoint of the viewer. Indeed, one of the major drawbacks of the "images of women" approach has been that the viewer seems to exist as nothing more than the miniature "mass public," eagerly and unthinkingly consuming the ideology that is being screened.
>
> The fundamental question . . . is how and why women like and enjoy the very films [in] which . . . our absence seems to be a precondition. Now we may know that women have always gone to the movies. But if a feminist reading against the grain does not take into account the ways in which female audiences have been constructed in the course of film history, then we risk developing a kind of tunnel vision that never sees much beyond the living rooms of contemporary feminist critics watching 1930s and 1940s movies on television.[17]

In other words, reading against the grain—refusing the explicit narrative that seems to insist on the subordination of women and reading instead secret subversions and protofeminist counternarratives—may be empowering but may overlook the (unequal) power of mass-produced imagery. A feminist critic may "read" *Dynasty* as an over-the-top, camp tale of active, sexual women, but this does not necessarily mean that the majority of women viewers will do so, or that the dominant meaning is not still resolutely patriarchal. Indeed, we must be careful not to "find" resistance and ideological slippage under every apparently hegemonic rock of popular culture, simply because we *want* it to be there. Feminist attention to narrative needs to traverse both these grounds—the ground of exposing the male-centered plots of popular culture as well as that of constructing alternative readings which tell a more empowering story.

One attempt to transcend this either/or bind—complete indoctrination by the narrative or complete rewriting—is through the use of the "encoding/decoding" model. Originally developed by Stuart Hall, a leading cultural theorist associated with the Centre for Contemporary Cultural Studies in England, this framework allows for a variety of interpretive possibilities. Hall's model describes three different positions a viewer could take. First is a reading of the image wholly within the dominant ideology; this first reading position would interpret the representation as it was "encoded" by the producers. Second is a "negotiated" reading, whereby one accepts the underlying framework of the ideology but challenges some of its particulars. Third is the "oppositional" reading, something like a reading against the grain where the viewer challenges the fundamental assumptions of the representation.[18] This encoding/decoding model has proved a useful, if incomplete, framework for many critical cultural studies. It allows for a more process-oriented understanding of the production and consumption of images, not forgoing the notion of a dominant ideology that is promoted in the text, but also not ignoring the multiple interpretive possibilities available to different social groups. This approach also has implications for how we think of the "spectator" (discussed in the next chapter).

Gender and Genre

These new, empowering stories created from readings against the grain have often been found in the analysis of specific forms of popular culture. More and more, feminist cultural critics have been interested in the relationship between gender and genre, between the construction of sexual difference and the specific signifying practices of a particular type of representation. The central question remains, Do some genres that have typically been presented for a female audience (melodramas, soap operas, romances) offer themselves up more than others to a feminist reading? Are there such things as "feminine forms" of representation and, if so, do they construct women differently? Is there a "female address" implied in many genres that focus on women's lives and women characters?

Much of this discussion about "female forms" has centered around film and television melodrama. In some ways, the new feminist concern with melodrama has historical and political aspects to it, because melodrama and "women's films," or the "weepies" as they were often called, have historically been seen as the "lowest" form of mass culture, not worthy of the critical attention paid male genres such as the Western or film noir. It is not surprising that genres associated both with a female audience and with "feminine" subject matters (the family, personal relationships, love, and so on) should be found unworthy of critical attention by male cultural critics: "According to the normative parameters of the ideology of mass culture, 'female' forms of 'mass culture' such as soap operas and popular romances are the lowest of the low, while 'male' genres such as detective and science fiction are considered able to rise above the low level of 'mass culture.'"[19] Feminist critics have reclaimed these films, television shows, and novels as worthwhile subjects for analysis, and some of the most provocative work in recent years (Tania Modleski's writings on romance, gothics, television soap operas, and Alfred Hitchcock; Janice Radway's study of female romance readers; Charlotte Brunsdon's work on British soap operas; and the excellent British Film Institute collection on melodrama) has derived from this attempt to deal with the question of gender and genre.

The study of soap operas has been central to the new feminist writings on genre, in particular those of Modleski, Dorothy Hobson, Brunsdon, and recent work by Martha Nochimson. The shift in orientation by these theorists is complex; they are not merely reclaiming a genre (largely watched by a female audience) for women spectators and critical analysis, but in fact arguing that soap operas, which appear so ridden with stereotypical and sexualized images of women, actually construct a positive space for the female viewer and for female subjectivity. Clearly, much of this work is in opposition to the hierarchies of critical analysis, in which "women's genres" are inevitably placed on the lowest rung, and where "women are . . . seen as the passive victims of the deceptive message of soap operas, just as the ideology of mass culture sees the audience as unwitting and pathetic victims of the commercial culture industry."[20] Countering this view, Nochimson, drawing heavily on the work of Modleski and others, asserts that "soap opera assumes an essential femininity and masculinity, but there the similarity ends, for soap opera looks with a critical eye at Hollywood's rigid interpretation of gender roles: women tucked securely under the influence of men. Hollywood fantasy is the fantasy of patriarchy. In soap opera, by contrast, another kind of yearning emerges, one rarely permitted expression in our culture. Soap opera includes a female subject."[21]

In *Loving with a Vengeance*, Modleski sees a feminist potential in television soap operas precisely because of their generic conventions and narrative structure, as does Annette Kuhn in her essay on women's genres: "Their characteristic narrative patterns, their foregrounding of 'female' skills in dealing with personal and domestic crises, and the capacity of their programme formats and scheduling to key into the rhythms of women's work in the home all address a female spectator."[22] Modleski sees a possibility in these genres for the creation of female "ways of seeing" that are not constrained by the male gaze and its associated dominance over female subjectivity. She even argues for the *radical* potential of forms such as the soap opera: "The disorder of the form conveys a structure of feeling appropriate to the experience of the woman in the home whose activities and concerns are dispersed and lacking a center. But precisely because of its decentered nature this most discredited genre can be aligned with advanced feminist aesthetics and advanced critical theory as a whole."[23]

Not only are soap operas structured like the rhythms of women's lives in the home, but the narrative content of most of these shows is the stuff of relationships, intimacies, sexuality, family—concerns often central to women and in contrast to the recent dominance of action/blockbuster films, where people are more likely to relate to cyborgs and dinosaurs than to each other. Furthermore, in daytime and nighttime soap operas women are more central as characters than in either "regular" television programming or Hollywood cinema. Women in soap operas are also able to traverse the rigid dichotomy of mother versus sexual woman that so often dominates both prime-time television and mainstream Hollywood; soap opera heroines are often mothers, lovers, and workers all at once.

Film melodrama has also come under close scrutiny because of the possibilities in a genre that both speaks to a female audience *and* foregrounds women in its "construction of narratives motivated by female desire and processes of spectator identification governed by female point-of-view."[24] Many feminist critics have argued that this highlighting of a female point of view renders the genre open to a feminist reading and available to a female audience: "Because the 'woman's film' obsessively centers and re-centers a female protagonist, placing her in a position of agency, it offers some resistance to an analysis which stresses the 'to-be-looked-at-ness' of the woman, her objectification as spectacle according to the masculine structure of the gaze."[25] The woman's film, or melodrama, is thus seen as a particular site of female agency and exploration and "is distinguished by its female protagonist, female point of view and its narrative which most often revolves around the traditional realms of women's experience: the familial, the domestic, the romantic—those arenas where love, emotion and relationships take precedence over action and events."[26] Not only can the melodrama invoke a female audience, but it can perhaps provoke a woman to resist the "resolution" that so often inscribes women in positions of subordination. Linda Williams's view "is not only that some maternal melodramas have historically addressed female audiences about issues of primary concern to women, but that these melodramas also have reading positions structured into their texts that demand a female reading competence. This competence derives from the different way women take on their identities under patriarchy and is a direct result of the social fact of female mothering."[27] Melodrama, then, is often seen in terms of its excess, its inability to fully enclose and recuperate the woman. It is in this excess and in the contradictions inherent in the subject of the genre (relationships, family, love, sex) that contestation can be located and analyzed.

Gledhill argues that melodrama must draw on the discourses of women's social reality in order for a female audience to be won over and that there is the possibility for contestation here: "In twentieth-century melodrama the dual role of woman as symbol for the whole culture and as representative of a historical, gendered point of view produces a struggle between male and female voices: the symbol cannot be owned, but is contested."[28] Jackie Byars echoes these concerns, emphasizing that melodramas may have a compensatory function but, at the same time, may also provide a space for female self-definition, precisely because of the centrality of women's lives to the "woman's film": "The narrative structure of the female-oriented family melodrama indicates the attempt to fill such a compensatory emotional function, the attempt to fulfil needs unmet in daily life. While this would seem to support the view that these are 'politically conservative' texts, it should be noted, following Radway, that they also function to transmit a 'female voice'—a vision of the world based in continuity rather than separation."[29]

Byars's book on family melodramas of the 1950s, *All That Hollywood Allows*, is a wonderful example of this kind of feminist genre criticism. In the best tradition of feminist interdisciplinary research, Byars traverses various approaches, using a revised psychoanalytic framework as well as historical and sociological models. While Byars recognizes clearly the extent to which these melodramas reinforced the dominant (gender, race, class) ideologies of the reactionary fifties, she also is able to show the places of indecision, the narrative inconsistencies, and the centrality of female desire and sexuality.

Melodramas, television soap operas, and other "women's genres" are therefore of interest to feminist critics for several reasons. Not only is there a possibility that these forms speak to—and thus help to construct—a female viewer, but they also deal thematically and narratively with issues that are central to women's lives. They frequently present a domestic world fraught with contradictions and struggles, and the "resolution" of these contradictions often appears tenuous at best.

Classically "female" forms have not been the only genres subject to feminist reexamination. There is a growing body of work that concerns those forms that seem most *unavailable* to a female audience. Mary Ann Doane's recent work on film noir attempts to analyze this most "male" genre:

> In the classical Hollywood cinema, there are two types of films within which the contradictions involved in the patriarchal representation of woman becomes most acute —melodrama and film noir. . . . What is particularly interesting about film noir for a feminist analysis is the way in which the issue of knowledge and its possibility or impossibility is articulated with questions concerning femininity and visibility. The woman confounds the relation between the visible and the knowable at the same time that she is made into an object for the gaze.[30]

Other feminists have examined gangster films and police shows in an attempt to locate questions of female identity in a broader generic context and to explore the contradictions in representations that explicitly deny women centrality and voice.

Feminist critics have hotly contested whether the contradictions opened up by these women's genres serve as progressive forces in women's lives or whether they are merely escape valves for women's frustrations and anxieties. For example, Ien Ang, who wrote a substantive study of the television series *Dallas*, argues that it is important not to assume that the acceptance of oppression in soap operas equals the acceptance of oppression in real life: "This acceptance (just like protest) takes place within the world of fantasy, not outside it. It says nothing about the positions and standpoints that the same women occupy in 'real life.' After all, watching soap operas is never the only thing they do. In other activities, other positions will be (or have to be) assumed."[31] The domesticity of the melodrama, however, might serve to mire women further in that realm as the only one available to them. In the next chapter, on spectatorship, we will explore these debates in detail.

4

You Looking at Me?
Seeing beyond the "Gaze"

Doing It for Ourselves:
Spectators and the Social Audience

This new discussion of female genres—melodrama, soap operas, the "woman's film"—has entailed a reevaluation of the female spectator and her possibilities in a patriarchal system of representation. The critique of psychoanalytic (textual) spectatorship theory did not issue from feminists alone. Indeed, a wide range of cultural theorists were involved in reconsidering the relationship between text and spectator. In many senses, this turn was part of a larger critique of formalism and textual analysis that entailed a shift in general cultural studies from effects studies to "uses and gratifications" research (itself marred by a reliance on survey techniques) and a movement toward the viewer. Narrative analysis, too, underwent a change of focus to a new consideration of the subjective aspect of filmgoing and the "effects" of narrative that was less text-based, more concerned with the audience, more concerned with social context, and less politically impartial. In other words, narrative analysis has shifted, and still is shifting, to extend into the process of producing meaning rather than analyzing the component parts of a structural unit. Overall, this has entailed a shift from positivist, quantitative audience research to more plural concepts of audiences and the production of meaning, signaling a move "away from an undifferentiated homogenous mass whose only significance is that it is watching television at any particular time to socially constituted audiences whose relationship with television involves the complex process of the production of meaning."[1]

As discussed in earlier chapters, many critics had difficulty with Mulvey's assertion of a monolithic male gaze. It not only presented a picture of a seamless web of patriarchal narrative, but also consigned women spectators to the unhappy positions of utter absence or self-negating masochism. As Betterton noted, "If the male look is characterized by voyeurism, observing and taking pleasure at a distance, the female look, it is claimed, is narcissistic, finding pleasure in closeness, in reflection and in identification with an image."[2] Disheartened by the rigidity and hopelessness of this paradigm, feminist critics began to reevaluate the concept of the gaze: "To say that women *can* and *do* look actively and erotically at images of men and other women disrupts the stifling categories of a theory which assumes that such a look is somehow always bound to be male."[3]

This reevaluation has taken many forms. First, there was the onslaught of questions directly challenging the concept of the gaze: Is it overly generalized? Is film really so monolithic? What about other visual media? Is it appropriate to use such deliberately psychoanalytic concepts to discuss the *social* process of filmgoing? Most important, what does this paradigm do for women? Is the gaze inevitably male? Are we forever condemned to consume images of our own objectification? Are we really structured as the "lack" that must be fetishized to reduce the threat posed by that lack? Do we not ourselves "gaze"? As Mary Ann Doane suggests, this rigid formulation of the spectator is problematic on a number of levels: "What has been elided in the conceptualization of the spectator is not only historical but sexual specificity. The spectator purportedly anticipated and positioned by the text, defined by the psychical mechanisms of scopophilia or voyeurism, fetishism and a primary mirror identification, is inevitably male."[4] Certainly, women *do* go to the movies, watch television, and listen to popular music, so how, E. Deidre Pribram asks, "have we come to perceive all forms of filmic gaze as male when women have always taken up their proportionate share of seats in the cinema? How have we come to understand cinematic pleasure (narrative, erotic, and so on) as pleasurable to the male viewer, but not the female? Why have we failed to see our own presence in the audience when women have always watched—and loved—film?"[5]

Feminist writing on audiences and spectatorship addresses questions central to power and resistance. Representations not only construct viewing positions but also construct subjectivities and identities. In addition, the particular social and cultural location of a viewer shapes and influences the way he or she "reads" a media text. This specific location is in turn implicated in a much larger social context that provides certain interpretive possibilities to the socially situated viewer.

If Mulvey's early psychoanalytic position claimed the impossibility of a female "look," trapped as we are by the male gaze and its attendant voyeurism, recent critics (including Mulvey herself in the essay rethinking "Visual Pleasure and Narrative Cinema"[6]) have attempted to find space for a female gaze, to open up this seemingly hermetically sealed relation between viewer and image, so as to avoid "contribut[ing] to the repression of the female gaze."[7]

The question of pleasure is central to this new dialogue around the gaze and spectatorship. As discussed in the previous chapter, narrative cinema was associated with a kind of pleasure that was both denigrating to and masochistic for women, a pleasure in our own objectification or a masculinized pleasure in which we are forced to lose our own subjectivity. Janet Bergstrom and Mary Ann Doane note, however, the significance of a critical shift in the field: "Whereas Mulvey theorized pleasure as a negative term, a mark of the subject's complicity with an oppressive sexual regime, for a host of others the term pleasure became a flag to rally around, offering the promise of a visual empowerment of women."[8] Indeed, one could reasonably argue that "pleasure" has become the new catchword of feminist cultural theory in an attempt to displace the emphasis on negative and oppressive images and construct instead a discourse that centers on the liberatory possibilities of female viewing practices and pleasures.

In the context of this discussion it is important to make a distinction between the terms *audience* and *spectator,* because not only are they tied to different intellectual traditions, but they are used quite differently in the analysis of representation and reception. The concept of audience is much more connected to the sociological tradition of communications research discussed earlier in this book. *Audience* refers, typically, to the actual people who sit and watch—who consume—a media production. The concept of spectator, particularly as it has been used by feminist film critics, refers to the *subject position* constructed by the representation. The spectator is not here a "real woman" but is instead a viewing position constructed by the signifying practice itself. The text constructs us *as spectators*, that is, as sites or locations for the enactment of specific psychic processes, such as voyeurism. These two modes of understanding the viewer and the viewing process have provoked much discussion and debate. Are we to focus on actual audiences, thus necessarily engaging in some sort of nontextual, empirical research? Or would we do better to read the cultural texts for what they imply about the people who are viewing them?

Annette Kuhn makes a distinction between the "social audience" as a "group of people who buy tickets at the box office, or who switch on the TV sets; people who can be surveyed, counted and categorized according to age, sex and socioeconomic status," and the "spectator," who is constructed in relation to the text.[9] This distinction entails profoundly different methodologies. Psychoanalytic critics impute or imply "spectator positions" from an analysis of the text because they believe that the text itself situates women and men in universal and repeatable ways. The text, therefore, remains central. Less psychoanalytically inclined theorists might engage in ethnographic audience research to ascertain how individuals or groups interpret and experience certain media events.

In many respects, the shift to the notion of "implied audience" or "implied spectator" or "imagined communities" (not always or necessarily psychoanalytically understood) was a response to the glib, quantitative research that was produced in the early audience studies, often called "effects" studies. This early audience research, unlike much of the sophisticated work of contemporary cultural ethnographers, was incapable of analyzing the media message itself, "merely grading it into lumps of *a priori* dangerous influence for categorization purposes."[10] The notion of an implied spectator allowed for extensive attention to the structural and ideological workings of the text under analysis. In this textual notion of spectatorship, a "spectator" will "read" an image according to his or her positioning by the textual operations.

Nevertheless, while this notion of implied spectator avoids the empiricism of the earlier concept of the audience member as a number to be counted, it has its own set of problems, as Ann Gray notes: "Such analyses have tended to assume an ideal (female) reader, inscribed within the feminine subject position offered by the text and further emphasised by the assumed cultural competencies of the reader. The risk inherent in this enterprise is the conflation of the 'implied' and the 'real' reader."[11] In other words, isn't it vital to maintain a distinction between how an actual woman experiences a cultural event and the assumption of how she will experience that event through a textual analysis? Gray and other critics have expressed concern over the possible conflation of these two "readers," a conflation that could result in a new kind of invisibility for the female consumer of popular culture.

Conversely, feminists interested in the "social audience" often engage in ethnographic research in which they interview women to ascertain exactly (or as exactly as possible, given the problems inherent in an interview situation or in conducting participant observation) how these women consume/interpret a representation and what they do in the process of making meaning out of it. These studies often owe a greater debt to anthropology and sociology than to textual literary criticism.

More recent work attempts to theorize an audience not

simply from the textual operations but from a social and historical analysis.[12] For example, one could draw on historical data, popular journalism, fan letters, production information, and other sources along with an analysis of the text (and perhaps interviews as well) to then presume certain kinds of viewing possibilities. In addition, there have been efforts to historicize the psychoanalytic conception of the spectator, effectively merging the conceptions of the spectator with those of the social audience member.

The debates about the different conceptions of female spectatorship remain central for feminist cultural criticism, as Rhona Berenstein notes: "There thus exists a tension between the female spectator conceived of as a product of the patriarchal system in which she is raised, the female spectator as a locus of the contradictions which compose her own personal life and her mediation of spectatorship, the female spectator as a psychoanalytic and/or ideological construct, and the female viewer which a film attempts to address but which may, in fact, not exist in the audience."[13] Recently theorists such as Jacqueline Bobo and Charlotte Brunsdon have challenged feminist cultural criticism to move beyond the de facto assumption of a white spectator and to address the multiple identities most of us hold. As Brunsdon says, we are "never 'just' gendered."[14]

Much of recent feminist writing about spectatorship is designed to "reclaim" or "recapture" popular texts for a feminist reader. Obviously, this work owes a debt to the practice of reading against the grain, discussed in the previous chapter. But it goes further, in that this counter-reading is done with explicit attention to the gender of that reader. In many cases, this approach involves rereading films or other representations that have been understood previously as exemplars of patriarchal filmmaking, including those of Hitchcock, as Jeanne Allen illustrates:

I will argue that the position of the female spectator, myself included, for *Rear Window* affords the pleasure of critically engaging the analysis of the traps and lures of heterosexual romance as presented by the constructed persona (not the historical person) "Hitchcock." The feminist spectator may view this film as an impetus for converting and transforming meaning in the discursive cinematic realm of the feminist critic. Having assessed the terms, the traps and lures in gender-based power struggle which *Rear Window* articulates, she may transform these terms into negotiation and convert a zero-sum proposition into an empathic compromise.[15]

Many writers have focused on those television shows, such as *Cagney and Lacey,* in which women's relationships are highlighted: "One of the main differences in the narrative gaze of *Cagney & Lacey* is that it seems to be a product of shared female experience in the workplace. The collective dimension of female experience is articulated, together with ideas of female friendship and solidarity. Such a range of looks—often fragmented and contradictory— perhaps more importantly constitutes an overall female perspective."[16] Lorraine Gamman argues further that this inscription of female lives into a typically male genre transforms the genre itself, rendering *Cagney and Lacey* (Figure 7) a different kind of cop show: "Representations of women with access to power—especially power unrelated to conspicuous consumption or ideologies of 'romance'—are quite uncommon in the mainstream. Positioning female characters as detectives in roles which show them 'thinking' and pursuing 'knowledge' without overdetermined reference to their physical competence or conventional 'attractiveness' is unusual."[17] Critics claim that a series like *Cagney and Lacey* actually inscribes or supports a female gaze both through its foregrounding of the cen-

Figure 7.   The dynamic duo of Cagney and Lacey challenges the conventions of the cop show and the strictures of women's lives. (CBS; photo courtesy of Photofest)

tral female characters and in its rewriting of the cop genre: "The 'female gaze' in *Cagney & Lacey* stems mainly from the point of view of the central female characters themselves, who articulate it via witty put-downs of male aspirations for total control. But in dismantling a masculinised notion of power, they don't automatically assume what in Lacanian theory has been described as the position of the 'Father.' On the contrary, they distance themselves from mastery."[18]

This area of feminist spectatorship analysis thus works within the terms of spectatorship set out by the psychoanalytic theorists in that it remains wedded to textual analysis, while at the same time tries to expand the terms of that analysis through specific attention to the possible

Figure 8.   Marilyn Monroe and Jane Russell enjoy each other's company in *Gentlemen Prefer Blondes*. (Twentieth Century Fox, 1953; photos courtesy of Photofest and Museum of Modern Art Film Stills Archive)

"reading positions" of women viewers. This work often draws on the literary model called "reader-response" theory, which "has questioned the objective and unchanging status of textual meaning and has provided the theoretical underpinnings for investigations of the cultural work accomplished by readers in interaction with texts."[19]

Much of the significance of the study of feminine forms and women's genres discussed in the previous chapter has to do with the possible "subject positions" they offer women spectators. For example, theorists as diverse as Modleski, Kuhn, and Jane Feuer have all argued that both "women's films" and the melodramatic television serial "seem to offer an especially active role for the spectator."[20]

In a stimulating essay on *Gentlemen Prefer Blondes* (Figure 8), a film that typically has been understood as an exemplar of voyeuristic male cinema, Lucie Arbuthnot and

Gail Seneca set out to "chronicle our search to understand our pleasure in this film."[21] The authors propose an empowering vision of the friendship between the two female characters (played by Jane Russell and Marilyn Monroe), which "invites the female viewer to join them, through identification, in valuing other women and ourselves."[22] They convincingly argue their case that the women in the film resist male objectification and in fact "return the look" both to the men in the film and, with love and respect, to each other, so that "we read, then, beneath the superficial story of heterosexual romance in *Gentlemen Prefer Blondes*, a feminist text which both denies men pleasure to some degree, and more importantly, celebrates women's pleasure in each other."[23]

Feminist work on spectatorship has also focused on the phenomena of stars and the fans who identify, imitate, adore, and revile them. Critics such as Richard Dyer and Christine Gledhill have asserted that a female gaze is activated or encouraged by the presence of certain kinds of female icons, such as Bette Davis, Katharine Hepburn, Marlene Dietrich, and, of course, Madonna. In her recent work on music videos, Lisa Lewis suggests that both Madonna and Cyndi Lauper "address girl audiences by textually making reference to consumer girl culture" in such a way that, in their mimicking of the rock stars, young girls play out "the stars' subversive stance against the femininity discourse and the privileging of male adolescence."[24] Lewis describes what she defines as two different sign systems that operate in the videos and self-presentation of these two stars: one allows girls access to typically male domains, such as the street, and the other directly references "distinctly female modes of cultural expression and experience,"[25] such as dressing up and shopping.

Figure 9.   Tough and sexy, masculinized and in control, Marlene Dietrich, Greta Garbo, and Bette Davis provide ample opportunities for lesbian spectators to fantasize and "desire differently." (Photos courtesy of Museum of Modern Art Film Stills Archive and Photofest)

The most provocative work on female stars and their
fans focuses on the possibilities of a "lesbian gaze"—a
theme explored by Andrea Weiss in her study of the space
for lesbian desire in watching such stars as Marlene Dietrich (especially when she kisses a woman in the cabaret
scene from *Morocco*), Bette Davis, Katharine Hepburn, and
Greta Garbo (Figure 9). Weiss argues that it is the com-
bination of the stars' extrafilmic personae (rumors
abounded about the lesbianism of both Dietrich and
Garbo) and the actual textual representations (the kiss in
the cabaret, the masculinized or androgynous attire) that
"provided an alternative model upon which lesbian spectators could draw."[26] Weiss explicitly challenges the psychoanalytic model of spectatorship as one that "can only
see lesbian desire as a function of assuming a masculine
heterosexual position"[27] and instead offers an analysis of
lesbian spectatorship that locates the lesbian filmgoer in
a social and historical context, a context of homophobia
both within and outside the film industry.

Revisioning Experience:
Feminism and the New Ethnography

The concern for discovering a female gaze or female spectator position has close links with a newly invigorated tendency toward ethnographic research. Bergstrom and
Doane point out that

> the problem, of course, was how to find out what these read-
> ing strategies were and where the subcultural resistance
> was located. Because the analyst's desire was somehow to
> construct a knowledge of the "other"—or more precisely,
> the other's knowledge—a resort to anthropological or soci-

ological methodologies seemed inevitable. This approach, which has come to be termed "ethnographic," makes use of such techniques as participant observation and audience interviews.[28]

For all the new work on a more mobile and complex notion of spectatorship, were we still too tied to analyzing this *thing*, this *text*? Worse yet, could it be that feminist textual analysis had replicated traditional patriarchal ways of seeing by privileging the discrete moment of image production outside of its social and experiential context? After all, the concept of "experience" has long been a touchstone for feminist scholarship. The turn to anthropological and sociological methodologies (interviews, participant observation, focus groups analysis, historical contextualization) emerged out of an attempt to uncover and interpret the nature of alternative reading strategies. It should be noted, too, that the psychoanalytic/semiotic approach and the ethnographic one, although not necessarily counterposed, do present significant opposition not only in methodology but also in epistemology, because, "for the ethnographer, the unconscious is not a pertinent factor. What he/she has access to are the conscious observations people make about the media, observations which the ethnographer may not take at face value but which are not subjected to a detailed scrutiny in view of the psychical strategies of disavowal, denegation and repression."[29]

Ethnographic research is certainly nothing new in the social sciences, but it does have a limited tradition in the analysis of mass media and popular culture. Most of the empirical work in cultural studies has, until recently, been quantitative and informed by conservative social theory. The British tradition of cultural studies, however, out of which many of the critical ethnographic studies grew, has consistently produced work that is deeply committed to an examination of how people experience their own cultural lives. Janice Radway stresses the importance of working with real audience perceptions, even though she is critical of an overreliance on the construction of "truth" through audience analysis: "Although our own interpretation as analyst is an inescapable, inevitable part of all mass culture research, it is nonetheless important and helpful to begin with a real audience's conscious, surface interpretation of a given form if we wish to understand how that form functions within the larger culture and, most especially, if we hope *ourselves* to contribute to the possibilities for challenging the material situation."[30] Radway, Ang, Brunsdon, Andrea Press, and others have all—in very different ways—attempted to extend beyond the limits of textual analysis and imputed spectator positions to understand how "real women" actually do engage with representations. Radway states that "the analytic focus must shift from the text itself, taken in isolation, to the complex social event of reading where a woman actively attributes sense to lexical signs in a silent process carried on in the context of her ordinary life."[31]

Indeed, Radway's work on women romance readers is a unique attempt to develop this framework in critical feminist practice. Radway's subjects (much like the male working-class subjects of earlier British research on subcultures) are neither duped consumers of cultural commodities nor simply enjoying themselves "innocently." They saw themselves as involved in a process with other women, a process that often allowed them respite from the requirements of husband and children. In that sense, these readers are doing more than simply escaping from the drudgery of housework; although their reading is, to some extent, compensatory, it also allows them to glimpse ways of life unlike their own and to question some of their assumptions and options. For example, the male characters in the romance novels, though often initially harsh and distant, frequently come around to express warmth and accessibility, attributes not often found among men in the "real lives" of the readers themselves. The women readers in Radway's study use romance novels in ways that are, contradictorily, helpful in negotiating their everyday existence and, ultimately, reproductive of that very existence.

Radway's insistence on blending the ethnographic and the textual, the anthropological and the psychoanalytic, broke down methodological barriers that had been firmly in place for years. Her attempt to integrate the critical and ethnographic impulses of a Birmingham-like perspective with a thorough feminist politics pointed to a lively set of research possibilities for feminist cultural critics. Her book "was less an account of the way romances as texts were interpreted than of the way romance reading as a form of behavior operated as a complex intervention in the ongoing social life of actual social subjects, women who saw themselves first as wives and mothers."[32] This perspective can begin to provide us with new and innovative ways of thinking about and doing cultural studies.

Much of contemporary television research follows Radway's model, exemplified by the recent collected volume *Television and Women's Culture*.[33] Dorothy Hobson, whose work on women and soap operas was central to these ongoing debates about both genre and female viewers, argues for a broadening out of the discussion, particularly around television research: "Television is a part of the everyday life of its audience. The way that women manage their time to fit their viewing into their domestic work has been discussed in many texts but there is much less information about the way that television comes into discussions outside the home and particularly in the workplace."[34] Hobson interviews women about their discussions of television in the workplace and concludes "that women use television programs as part of their general discourse on their own lives, the lives of their families and friends and to add interest to their working lives. It adds to the critique of audiences as passive viewers by putting forward the hypothesis that it is the discussion after television programs have been viewed which completes the process of communication and locates television programs as part of popular culture."[35]

Hobson and others, such as Radway, have also asserted that their research indicates that reading romances—or watching soap operas—is not merely, or only, a compensatory activity that further mires women in the muck of patriarchal domination. Both Radway and Hobson point out that "the use of events within fiction to explore experiences which were perhaps too personal or painful to talk about to a complete work group is a beneficial and creative way of extending the value of the program into their own lives."[36]

Many other feminists have used ethnographic methods to determine these different reading positions. Jacqueline Bobo conducted group interviews to analyze the reception and interpretation of the film *The Color Purple*, "to examine the way in which a specific audience creates meaning from a mainstream text and uses the reconstructed meaning to empower themselves and their social group."[37] Drawing on Stuart Hall's theory of encoding/decoding, as well as film historical analysis that locates this particular film in a larger context of films about African Americans made by white male directors, Bobo paints a picture of a complex process whereby members of an African-American audience bring to the film a knowledge of the stereotypes that will be employed and then (consciously or unconsciously) negotiate with those images to glean something for themselves: "Given the similarities of *The Color Purple* to past films that have portrayed Black people negatively, Black women's positive reaction to the film seems inconceivable. However, their stated comments and published reports prove that Black women not only like the film but have formed a strong attachment to it. The film is significant in their lives"[38] (Figure 10). Bobo continues to place this reception in the context of "cultural competencies" surrounding the emergence of a "canon" of African-American women writers: "Black women's response to the film *The Color Purple* is not coincidental, nor is it insignificant. It is in keeping with the recent emergence of a body of critical works about the heritage of Black women writers, the recent appearance of other novels by Black women written in the same vein as *The Color Purple* and, very importantly, the fact that there is a knowledgeable core of Black women readers of both literary and filmic texts."[39]

This notion of "cultural competencies" has proven to be compelling. Developed originally by David Morley in his pioneering ethnographic studies of television viewers in England, this concept insists that people enter into the viewing situation with a host of skills and interpretive maneuvers; Shaun Moores notes that "while recognizing the text's construction of subject positions for the spectator, Brunsdon and Morley pointed to readers as the possessors of already-constructed cultural knowledges and competencies which are drawn on at the moment of interpretation."[40] In other words, people do not enter into any viewing situation as neutral, empty vessels, waiting to be filled by the

Figure 10.   A dubious adaptation of Alice Walker's moving *The Color Purple* found an appreciative audience despite the film's obvious flaws. (Warner Brothers, 1985; photo courtesy of Museum of Modern Art Film Stills Archive)

particular message emanating from the movie screen or the television set. Rather, we are accompanied by complex histories, knowledges, and interpretive skills that are brought into play as we engage with particular kinds of images.

Constance Penley's wonderful work on women *Star Trek* fans is, like Bobo's study of *The Color Purple*, exemplary ethnographic research.[41] Penley studied women fans who participate in the world of "zines"—self-produced fan magazines that expand on and reconstruct the world of *Star Trek*. She focused on women who wrote/drew what are known as "slash zines," stories that rewrite the characters Dr. Spock and Captain Kirk as lovers. Her study presents a complex analysis of the ways in which "everyday women" use and reinterpret popular cultural forms that draws on a variety of methodological techniques, including participant observation (at a "zine" conference), semiotic/textual analysis, psychoanalysis, and interviews.

Studies such as Penley's broaden our definition of "reception," for they enlarge the context of reception beyond the moment of viewing and "reading" to a larger circuit of engagements that include discussing the shows with one's friends and family: "By not asking merely, What do people do with the text? (stop) but, What do they do with the text *in the real world*?, a way is offered for 'audience' to mean more than merely receiver or reader of others' encodings."[42] Here, "subject positions" are not wholly determined by the signifying apparatus, but are contested and struggled over by actual women in the process of reading/viewing/consuming: "While we have known for a long time how popular culture seems to secure the dominant interests of the ruling elites and facilitates consent and control among people, it is only recently that we have started to ponder how popular media forms might also offer the possibilities for a resistance away from a rigidly defined and controlled patriarchal definition of feminine subjectivity."[43]

In an article on images of women's bodybuilding, Laurie Schulze discusses the transition from text-based analysis to a new concern with the spectator as active constructor of meaning. Critiquing Hall's conception of "preferred reading" as setting up a situation in which "the text [is] still taking precedence over readings that might be made of it,"[44] she invokes Morley's use of the term *relevance*, whereby "the reader produces meanings and pleasures 'that are relevant to his or her social allegiances at the moment of viewing— the criteria for relevance *precede* the viewing moment.'"[45] As Schulze notes, the "move from preference to relevance is emblematic of recent efforts in cultural studies to pull farther away from a text-centric criticism that privileges textual structures and the subjectivity that the text is supposed to construct, towards a retheorization of texts and readers that, as Fiske says, breaks down both the notions of the stable text and the stable audience."[46]

Kuhn echoes these concerns when she too discusses female bodybuilding in an analysis of audience response to the 1985 film *Pumping Iron II: The Women*. Kuhn attended a rare all-women screening of the film, which prompted some insights about the possibilities of pleasure for female spectators derived from the film's exploration of strong and powerful female bodies.[47] Yet Kuhn, unlike some of the other critics discussed here, insists that these pleasures are, in fact, "to be seduced by these operations; to be subject to, to submit to, the powers they inscribe. . . . She/he is positioned, defined, set in place, within these powers and constructs."[48] So the pleasure here, for Kuhn, is really like a drop of (narcissistic) resistance in a sea of fetishization.

The discussion of female spectatorship has been particularly fruitful around questions of sexual identity and lesbian spectatorship. Elizabeth Ellsworth writes about how feminist reviewers "appropriated *Personal Best* into oppositional spaces constructed by feminist political practice"[49] in order both to challenge dominant meanings and to help construct a shared, collective space for a feminist subjectivity (Figure 11). Ellsworth found that lesbian-feminist reviewers deliberately and boldly rewrote and redefined this film to such an extent that they "named and eroticized" moments in the film. Identification and empowerment were achieved not through a simple reading against the grain but rather through a complex process that utilized the preexisting cultural codes of lesbian culture to

Figure 11.   Lesbian audiences and critics rewrite the heterosexist resolution of *Personal Best.* (Warner Brothers, 1981; photo courtesy of Museum of Modern Art Film Stills Archive)

"bring out" and validate the lesbianism that appears to be defeated in the film's overt narrative.

Television has provided fertile ground for feminist ethnographic research. After Dan Quayle upped the ante of election-year rhetoric by railing against prime time's favorite single mother, Murphy Brown, academics would be foolish to ignore the impact of television on the media-saturated body politic. Indeed, in recent years the convergence of feminist cultural studies with television studies has produced a burgeoning new literature on women and television, particularly surrounding questions of spectatorship and consumption.

No longer satisfied to treat female spectators as simple receivers of a (unified) cultural message, feminist television critics have attempted to develop models of reception that locate the viewer in a particular history—with an ethnicity, a sexual identity, a class position, and so on. In this way, cultural products are understood not as a unified field of impenetrable ideology but as a complex array of competing and contradictory discourses that, while generally reinforcing dominant power relations, often provide space for resistance and contestation. Television, that peculiarly home-based and domestic medium, has provided fertile ground for this exploration of the social relations of consuming/viewing mass-produced images.

Private Screenings: Television and the Female Consumer, a collection of essays edited by Lynn Spigel and Denise Mann, emerged from the pioneering feminist journal *Camera Obscura*. This collection represents the latest example of feminist cultural criticism—a heady mixture of substantive historical studies, innovative reception analyses, and sophisticated textual work. The nine chapters (and a final helpful television source guide) focus on everything from early television to *Cagney and Lacey*, yet manage to connect as a whole better than most anthologies. All the contributors share a consistent concern with, as the editors put it, "the way television tries to appeal to women consumers and the way it inserts itself into their everyday lives, both at home and at the marketplace."[50] Most of the essays attend to close historical analysis, placing particular texts and cultural moments in a specific social location. This close analysis often entails what I call an intertextual approach: the authors draw on a wide array of sources, including fan letters, advertising, production notes, industrial data, popular magazine articles, architectural developments, and other sociocultural information. This wide-ranging approach imparts a richness and texture to the topics being analyzed and effectively demonstrates the by now axiomatic principle of cultural studies as a multilayered project.

For example, Aniko Bodroghkozy, in a chapter on the politics of race and gender in the 1960s sitcom *Julia*, effectively analyzes the competing discourses of a series that attempted to address television's racist past yet refused to reckon with the civil rights challenges of its own time. Drawing on production notes from *Julia* scripts, letters to the producers from both African-American and white viewers, and popular press discussions, Bodroghkozy places *Julia* in a historical context that identifies it as a "symptomatic text" that spoke contradictorily about both race and gender.

Similarly, Lynn Spigel's essay "Installing the Television Set," on the selling of television to the postwar family, uses multiple sources in constructing a complex picture of the ambivalence produced by television and its sponsors. Like so many of the authors in this collection, Spigel sees television's origins as fundamentally contradictory; Americans embraced television as the familial and suburban link to a brave new world of mass images and mass consumption, yet simultaneously feared its invasion of domestic space, as it configured new (gendered) relations between consumerism, family life, and popular images. Other chapters include incisive work on melodrama, television variety shows, Hollywood stars, and early television's depiction of class and ethnicity.

Andrea Press's *Women Watching Television: Gender, Class, and Generation in the American Television Experience* is a book of a different order. While ostensibly concerned with the same general topic—women and television—Press focuses on consumption in a more traditional sense: the interpretation of the images and narratives of television. In addition, she is writing more generally about women's experience of television, a marked departure from the small-scale but thorough studies found in the Spigel and Mann volume.

Press is to be commended for her effort to transcend the limiting paradigms of so much recent cultural criticism, which often emphasizes class at the expense of gender, or vice versa. Methodologically, she is innovative as well, attempting to combine a historical analysis of television's representation of women and social class with the richness of women's own interpretations of their experiences of television. Although this effort to address the "big picture" is admirable (and one with which I am sympathetic), it runs into the inevitable problems of overgeneralization and theoretical weakness. Nevertheless, Press presents an insightful look at the impact of class and generation on women's experience of television, giving substantive analytic weight to the commonsense assertion that women of different classes and different ages negotiate with the mass media in distinct ways. Interestingly, Press concludes that questions of realism and identification are central to the discrepancies between working- and middle-class television experiences, working-class women responding more to television's purported realism and middle-class women engaging more with issues of identification and character.

While I am largely in agreement with Press's theoretical framework (a model drawing strongly on the work of the Birmingham Centre for Contemporary Cultural Studies, which attempts to join the possibility of viewer resistance while attending to the hegemony of dominant images), I find her book tentative in its conclusions. Again, this is not so much a fault of Press's methodology or theoretical model; rather, it is often the case that such large-scale endeavors lack a certain precision that more limited studies exhibit.

As both *Women Watching Television* and *Private Screenings* indicate, television may indeed have "its eye on women," but we do not just stare at the screen blankly, accepting its versions of female subjectivity as the only available options. We resist, reinterpret, willfully read against the grain, and reinscribe dominant meanings with our own subversive interpretations. Both books add a great deal to the growing field of feminist cultural studies.

These newer developments in feminist cultural theory are promising, because they begin to offer a way out of the unsatisfying options of empiricism or textual analysis. Kuhn and other critics have tried to bridge this gap between the different conceptions of the "female spectator," discussed earlier, by seeing them as part of a continuum in which the construction of one is dependent upon the other: "Social audiences become spectators in the moment they engage in the processes and pleasures of meaning-making attendant on watching a film or TV programme. The anticipated pleasure of spectatorship is perhaps a necessary condition of existence of audiences. In taking part in the social act of consuming representations, a group of spectators becomes a social audience."[51] Women's genres, then, can be said to address both a social audience of women (marketing to people who are already constructed as women) and a feminine spectator: "If soaps and melodramas inscribe femininity in their address, women—as well as being already formed *for* such representations—are in a sense also formed *by* them."[52]

Although this new attention to the "female gaze" is to be lauded, it holds the danger of overlooking the often violent reality of male domination and male objectification of women in images. The motivation for much of this spectatorship (or female gaze) theory is to move us away from situating women as complete victims, determined entirely

by the totalistic male gaze and therefore unable to do anything but consume our own objectification—an uninspir-
ing position to be sure. Female gaze theory attempts to
locate resistance in women's ways of seeing images and
constructing meaning. In addition, it tries to give substantive weight to the theoretical position that meaning is
not just apparent in the text but is actively made in an interaction between viewer and image.

This is a necessary and commendable move, yet we must
remain aware of the institutional and representational strictures placed on our experience of popular culture. Women
certainly are not the passive viewers cultural theory often
has made us out to be; however, we are also not free to create resistant reading out of whole cloth. Images are so often
filled with dominant cultural messages that, while a few
women may read radically against the grain, the vast
majority of us will feel the weight of the dominant ideology and interpret the codes without much semiotic play.
Ann Gray alerts us to the dangers of an overly celebratory
approach: "What seems to be happening here, and it is a
worrying trend, is that by celebrating on the one hand an
active audience for popular forms and on the other those
popular forms which the audience 'enjoy,' we appear to be
throwing the whole enterprise of a cultural critique out of
the window."[53]

In her exciting essay "Banality in Cultural Studies,"
Meaghan Morris challenges some of this "new thinking"
in cultural studies, both for its repetitiveness—"I get the
feeling that somewhere in some English publisher's vault
there is a master disk from which thousands of versions
of the same article about pleasure, resistance, and the politics of consumption are being run off under different
names with minor variations"—and for its often glib

adherence to a notion of "the people": "What takes its place is first, a citing of popular voices (the informants), an act of translation and commentary, and then a play of *identification* between the knowing subject of cultural studies and a collective subject, 'the people.'"[54]

Ethnographic research—and an emphasis on varying interpretive possibilities—can empower women, but it can lead to a wishy-washy pluralism where "people in modern mediatized societies are complex and contradictory, mass cultural texts are complex and contradictory, therefore people using them produce complex and contradictory culture."[55] It can also be used as "evidence" of a "truth" that somehow appears unmediated. It is vital to remember that even an ethnographic approach involves a great deal of interpretation on the part of the critic; interviews do not present wholesale truths any more than another methodology might.

In addition, as Jacqueline Bobo and Ellen Seiter have pointed out, ethnographic research is marred by the same overweening focus on white women's lives from which other feminist research has suffered. These authors note that the new emphasis on ethnographic television studies in homes (to elaborate the domestic context of television viewing) ignores the social structure of the interviewer / interviewee situation, in which, given the racial politics of academia, the interviewer is likely to be white and therefore not easily taken into the home of a respondent of color.[56]

The question is, Who/what has the power to determine meaning? Is it the viewer—who makes of the image what she will—or is it the image itself that determines certain readings from the viewers? Christine Gledhill, in her important contribution to the *Female Spectators* volume, argues for the use of the term *negotiation* to replace both the reflectionist models of "images of women" perspectives and the determinism and ahistoricism of "cine-psychoanalysis":

> The term "negotiation" implies the holding together of opposite sides in an ongoing process of give-and-take. As a model of meaning production, negotiation conceives cultural exchange as the intersection of processes of production and reception, in which overlapping but non-matching determinations operate. Meaning is neither imposed, nor passively imbibed, but arises out of a struggle or negotiation between competing frames of reference, motivation and experience.[57]

Gledhill goes on to state that we negotiate at every level, from the institutional level where organized feminists put pressure on the various media institutions (for example, the *Cagney and Lacey* case) to negotiations over the meaning of texts to the active process of reception. As Gledhill notes, taking as a starting point the reception of various social audiences is not without a host of problems:

> Such an approach is open to charges of relativism—in other words, there is no point to ideological analysis because meaning is so dependent on variable context. Or it may be accused of populism—a media product cannot be critiqued if audiences demonstrably enjoy it. . . . And concern with the pleasures or identifications of actual audiences seems to ignore the long-term task of overthrowing dominant structures, within which resistant or emergent voices struggle on unequal terms.[58]

In other words, we need to ask what women *do* with all this resistance, how they use it and work with it in their everyday lives; Press stresses that "if women's tendency to resist hegemony through creative interpretations of television truly stops in the kitchen, then this evidence of resistance must be counted as something else. Theorists of resistance must develop some means for assessing the political effectiveness of the resistance they chronicle."[59] This is the crucial issue, for "resistance"—if it is to have any meaning at all—must be concerned with changing the social conditions of women's lives. As Jackie Byars notes, "Feminists have a greater motivation than many other theorists to link the theoretical and the practical, and as a result, this distinction between discursive subject and social-historical subject has proved especially problematic."[60] Byars then asks the central questions, questions that have come to dominate the most recent work in feminist cultural studies:

> Primarily, what is the relation between the "social" spectator and the spectator positioned by the text? Additionally, what is the relation between the spectator and film form? How does identification work? How do the unconscious desires of the spectator influence interpretation? How much control can a spectator exert over her or his interpretation? How can we account for the existence of varying indefensible feminist readings of a text? And, especially important for feminists, is spectatorship gendered?[61]

For all these cautionary provisos, the latest work in female spectatorship bodes well for feminist cultural studies. In its multilayered and intertextual approach, it begins to break down the stubborn barriers between the ethnographic and the ideological, the contextual and the textual, production and reception. In so doing, this exciting work challenges us to reckon with the complexity and variability of women's experiences of popular culture.

5

Postfeminism and Popular Culture
A Case Study of the Backlash

This chapter could aptly be subtitled "Whose Life Is It Anyway? Fatal Retractions in the Backlash 1980s." Or, one is Presumed Innocent until a Pretty Woman causes a Fatal Attraction that makes a Working Girl into a Ghost. If this is postfeminism, then June Cleaver is Gloria Steinem; postmodern simulation notwithstanding, I don't think she is.

This chapter explores the images of the backlash, a term made famous by Susan Faludi's 1991 bestselling book of the same name. Faludi brilliantly charts the backlash against feminism and, while spending several chapters on the cultural images of this backlash, is far more eloquent in her denunciation of the larger social forces that shaped antifeminism in the 1980s. Here I focus more explicitly on those media representations that were and still are so much a part of this backlash and, in doing so, "model" a certain kind of feminist cultural analysis that I have been implying since the opening incursion into the territory of Madonna, *Thelma and Louise,* and *Murphy Brown.*

This chapter traces the development of a cultural

"moment"—a convergence of various discourses (film, television, advertisements, popular journalism, public policies, academic trends) that produce a particular sensibility or ethos. This approach is not meant to imply that the backlash is all-encompassing or without contradictions, or that it affects all people in the same way or with equal force. No cultural period is ever singular in its expression of ideologies, and I hint at some of those contradictions in this chapter. Nevertheless, the 1980s and early 1990s did exhibit what we might call "dominant ideologies" about women, women's lives, women's options, women's choices. I choose to link these discourses under the banner term *postfeminism* because I believe this word encompasses the backlash sentiment already mentioned as well as a more complex phenomenon of a recent form of antifeminism.

This chapter is not, however, intended as the "final statement" either on this historical period or on feminist cultural methodology. Rather it is intended to present a loose case study in order to make specific and substantive points about a cultural moment or epoch, as well as to demonstrate a way of undertaking feminist cultural studies that is contextual, intertextual, historical, and motivated by explicit feminist questions and concerns.

Currently two strands of what we could call "postfeminist" discourse exist. In recent years, postfeminism has emerged both as a descriptive popular category and as a tentative theoretical movement loosely associated with the postmodern and poststructuralist challenge to "identity politics."[1] These two versions of postfeminism (the popular, mainstream backlash one and the one associated with academic poststructuralism and postmodernism) have serious points of overlap that equally, albeit with different intentions, contribute to the dissolution of feminism as theory *and* practice. The term *postfeminism* was probably first used in public discourse in an October 1982 *New York Times Magazine* cover article titled "Voices from the Post-Feminist Generation" written by Susan Bolotin, a feminist bemoaning the state of regressive womanhood and feeling all too anachronistic in this postfeminist world. In her interviews with young women, one characteristic stands out clearly—the way these women view feminists: "Look around and you'll see some happy women, and then you'll see these bitter, bitter women. The unhappy women are all feminists. You'll find very few happy, enthusiastic relaxed people who are ardent supporters of feminism. Feminists are really tortured people."[2]

Time magazine declared on its cover of December 1989 that "in the 80s they tried to have it all. Now they've just plain had it. Is there a future for feminism?" The answer is pretty grim, because "hairy legs haunt the feminist movement, as do images of being strident and lesbian. Feminine clothing is back; breasts are back; motherhood is back."[3] One would think that in the sinister 1970s, we all wore Hefty bags, cut our breasts off, and had our tubes summarily tied. The linking of feminism with cultural signifiers of "difference" (lesbianism), which then become conflated with fashion (hairy legs), is an ideological sleight of hand that plays into the worst sort of egregiously sexist stereotyping. Counterposed to this imaginary vision of mean and hairy lesbians is the "new woman" of the late 1980s and the 1990s: a woman whose essence is neatly encapsulated by reference to fashion (feminine clothing), body parts (breasts), and reproductive institutions (motherhood). Claudia Wallis, author of the *Time* story, tellingly characterizes feminism via the media-concocted mythology of the Superwoman: "What happened to the superwoman in the tailored suit and floppy bow tie who brought home all that bacon? What happened to breakfast with the national sales manager and racing for the 8:05? What happened to aspiring to the executive suite, to beating men at their own game?"[4] Not only does this description falsely circumscribe feminism as solely concerned with equality on the job, but its classism boils over and glibly permeates the entire article. The false dichotomies are rigidly presented: Superwoman versus mother, strident lesbian versus mellow and "feminine" heterosexual; unattractive bra-burner versus smartly attired accessorizer. Of course, neither side of the dichotomy rings true; each is, in its own way, fully ideological.

Popular postfeminism is therefore predictably located within the generalized antifeminist backlash that has been given free rein in the past ten years. Sources as diverse as the *New York Times*, the film *Baby Boom*, bestsellers about "career women gone wrong," and television series about troubled single women (such as the brief recent series *The Trials of Rosie O'Neill*) present a somewhat contradictory image of a movement devoid of currency and at the same time responsible for the sad plight of millions of unhappy and unsatisfied women who, thinking they could have it all, have clearly "gone too far" and jeopardized their chances at achieving the much valorized American Dream. This discourse, like so many others before it, has declared the movement (predictably if illogically) dead, victorious, and ultimately failed. In so doing, this popular view of feminism has rewritten the history of the women's movement to shift it from the terrain of well-intentioned and earnest docudrama to that of smarmy tabloid-style television reenactments on *A Current Affair.*

In this time of backlash and revisionism, the popular narrative of the history of the contemporary women's movement unfolds like this: In the beginning . . . our newly awakened anger and astonishment at the realities of our own oppression caused us to take positions that were extreme. We went too far, either becoming "like men" in our quest for acceptance or finding ourselves doing double duty at home and work. One of these "extreme" positions was the radical rethinking of motherhood as the sole fulfilling role for the adult woman.[5] But as the popular historians would have it now, we have emerged from the dark, angry nights of early women's liberation into the bright dawn of a postfeminist era. The personal history of feminist pioneer Betty Friedan is instructive. In her first, groundbreaking book, *The Feminine Mystique*,[6] Friedan bemoaned the state of the American woman, overeducated for the menial and unfulfilling role of housewife/mother that was forced on her with vigor since the end of World War II. Friedan urged women into the workforce and careers as the only way to develop fully and liberate themselves. Her words spoke to a generation of women who felt some vague malaise, sensed a grave injustice, but were unable to find a voice for it, a name for it: sexism. By the early 1980s, however, Friedan was singing another tune, wondering aloud if we had not, perhaps, gone a bit too far, bemoaning now not the state of imprisoned womanhood, but the sorry lack of family life. After all, she seemed to ask, isn't motherhood (and its associated ideological baggage—heterosexuality, couplehood, the nuclear family) what women really want? In *The Second Stage*[7] Friedan fully recanted and railed against those feminists who still thought that the family was a central site of women's oppression. In her most recent backtracking, Friedan continues to blame the women's movement for "excesses" that resulted in an unfortunate "war" with men.

For Friedan and others (such as 1993 cover-girl antifeminist Katie Roiphe), we may have come a long way (baby) but we still have a long way to go (back). This era, we are

told, has its own set of problems. We are being punished
for wanting it all: the Superwoman syndrome and the Cinderella complex are the watchwords that construct a
female identity in crisis, a subjectivity at war with its own
history, a woman bereft. As popular wisdom would have
it, contemporary women are now caught in the binds their
foremothers unwittingly made for them: in renouncing traditional values of Mom and apple pie (especially Mom),
today's woman is a lost soul, an ambitious career woman
who has lost touch with that essential part of her female-
ness—motherhood.

Feminism, that tired relic of the turbulent 1960s and
early 1970s, like a high-budget miniseries, promised more
than it put out. We thought we wanted liberation, but we
found out that we really love too much. We thought we
wanted equality, but realize instead that we cannot have
it all. We thought we could finally be the prince in our own
fantasies of power and pleasure, but discover our Cinderella
complex weighs on us all too mightily. We envisioned co-
operation, commitment, even community, but are told we
are codependent after all. If this is postfeminism, then
Barbara Bush is Alice Walker.

More pointed attacks on the perils of a feminist identity can be seen in many television specials, particularly
those that focus on family relations. One program, *Supermom's Daughter*, stands out dramatically because it seems,
on first viewing, to resonate with many ideas of the feminist movement. This program borrows from feminism
selectively, however, and in doing so presents an ideological orientation that is infinitely more subtle in its sexism than, say, *Father Knows Best*. In this Home Box Office
special, star television news reporter Mom is horrified to
learn that her teenage daughter has swerved off the academic fast track and is instead intent on achieving an early

marriage, producing lots of children, and working in early childhood education. The worst nightmare of every feminist mother comes true: her daughter wants nothing of the life she has struggled to make available to her.

Significantly, a television show like this locates itself firmly in the ideological framework of the 1980s (and the 1990s as well), which presents an image of troubled womanhood, of striving career women suddenly faced with the deep truth of their bottomless need for hearth and home, husband and children. In this age of *Fatal Attraction* and *Baby Boom,* feminist struggles and gains are reduced to personal choices, choices that, we are now informed, have created a no-win situation: we cannot have it all.

The intention of numerous 1980s films, television shows, and other forms of popular culture is precisely this: to further dichotomize mother and woman, with an additional postfeminist gloss by identifying "woman" not only as sexual, but as ambitious Superwoman. The "you can't have it all" issue emerges specifically as a response to real and substantive feminist changes in the workplace and in social and personal life. The Supermom of the television show confides to her housewife friend (and idol of her daughter) that she often envies her friend's domestic life, and the friend appropriately returns the compliment, thus reinforcing the work/family dichotomy that has come to be defined as the crucial postfeminist issue.

The major postfeminist paradigm has precisely been this work/family duality, which condemns feminism for helping to create the double-day/second-shift syndrome, yet completely overlooks a more radical critique of either work or family. The much vaunted "juggling" of work and family has become the subject of endless talk shows, sitcoms, films, popular articles, and glossy advertisements. A recent piece on an *NBC Nightly News* show depicted the creative solution of a "working mother" (a redundant term, to be sure) who had negotiated the rigors of family and work conflicts by working part time at her Wall Street firm. The entire segment never made any mention of this work/family dilemma as a problem for men, but presented it rather as a problem that women could now work out with the paternalistic help of benign and benevolent corporate America.

Geneva Overholser, in a *New York Times* editorial of September 1986, notes that "among most people who use the term 'post-feminism' there seem to be two schools of thought. The first holds that women went rampaging off to work only to discover that they were cheating home and family. The second holds that women went rampaging off to work only to discover that work wasn't so great after all."[8] Overholser convincingly argues that the term *post-feminism* is simply sexism by a subtler name.

Several popular films of the late 1980s speak to this new dialogue of female angst. In *Fatal Attraction* (Figure 12), the bad woman is the childless, single, professional woman who seduces the innocent family man and tellingly attempts to blackmail him with a fantasized pregnancy. The good woman is, like in old times, the good *mother*, who significantly is a sophisticated housewife. The figure of evil here is a single woman, living in the hell-like neighborhood of Manhattan's meat district, who smokes, has wild blonde hair, and whose "biological clock" is ticking rather like a timebomb. She is a homewrecker: she kidnaps a young girl, boils her pet bunny, and looks in on the couple's domestic bliss and throws up. She is clearly the "working woman from hell," beloved of recent popular culture, who gets her comeuppance when she is finally "put away" (to cheers from audiences throughout the country) by the dutiful wife and mother.

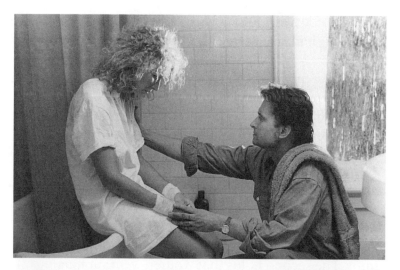

Figure 12. Things go from bad to worse in *Fatal Attraction*, the misogynist emblem of 1980s antifeminism. (Paramount, 1987; photos courtesy of Photofest)

Figure 13.   Business executive Diane Keaton cannot get the hang of mothering in *Baby Boom*, a backlash trifle. (United Artists, 1987; photo courtesy of Museum of Modern Art Film Stills Archive)

Diane Keaton in *Baby Boom* (Figure 13) lets us all know the deep dissatisfaction of women at work and lays bare the budding mama lurking behind every gleaming corporate desk. Keaton's enactment of a corporate executive whose nascent maternal instinct is aroused, leading her to the country and marriage, is only one, lighthearted example of the consequences meted out to women who fail to fit into their appropriately gendered positions.

In *Working Girl* (Figure 14), an example of what I call the "executive in a G-string theme," Tess, the striving working-class woman, tells us in perfect postfeminist prose that she has "a mind for business and a bod for sin." The good merger man Jack Trainer saves her from the evils of a female (masculinized and corrupt) boss, and the Pyrrhic feminist victory is reduced to Tess's commitment

Figure 14.   The sexy secretary gets the job and the man (and gets to keep her "femininity") in the pseudofeminist *Working Girl.* (Twentieth Century Fox, 1988; photo courtesy of Photofest)

to get her own coffee when she is rewarded with a management position and a female secretary. The bad woman here is the woman executive who has lost her "true" womanly ways in her climb up the corporate ladder.

The immensely popular film *Pretty Woman* (Figure 15) is emblematic of the postfeminist genre. A glitzy reworking of the classic Cinderella tale, *Pretty Woman* offers yet another backlash dystopia: a world where women are whores with warm hearts of gold and men are rich corporate raiders with organs in need of thawing by those selfsame hearts. Among commentators it even became a point of pride to admit, as did *Hers* columnist Daphne Merkin in the *New York Times*, the "illicit affection for a glossy cinematic fairy tale about a prostitute and a highrolling businessman." To be critical of such a regressive film is to be, in Merkin's words, "inheritors of the feminist

Figure 15.   In *Pretty Woman*, the man buys his pretty woman and then "earns" her love—a retro film for the retro Reagan-Bush years. (Touchstone, 1991; photo courtesy of Museum of Modern Art Film Stills Archive)

mystique" who "felt compelled to protest the choice of Barbara Bush as a commencement speaker."[9] Merkin reiterates the reconstructed narrative of feminist history by arguing that we have, indeed, gone too far and now need to realize that, instead of the vision of liberated singledom in *An Unmarried Woman*, women adore the fantasy of the male savior, of the knight in shining armor. In this reading, women's fantasies (and men's too, for that matter) are intractable and, try as we might, we are misguided souls if we think we can escape these universal models of domination and submission, transformation and surrender: "It appears that in the post-modernist, post-feminist, closing decade of the 20th century, we still need our myths, our amatory fictions; they help us endure. We are ready again for the mad, implausible embrace."[10]

Once we were highly critical of the delusive fictions that

helped us "endure" the pains of patriarchy. It used to be we constructed alternative fantasies of pleasure and passion, which deconstructed that endurance and helped to develop a changing social body. But in this postfeminist backlash, passion is the province of prefeminist, timeless yearnings that were only slightly derailed by that irksome challenge to patriarchal business as usual: "By deliberately announcing itself as fairy tale, *Pretty Woman* succeeds in bridging the contradiction faced by the spectator who is no longer able to believe in romance (especially in a film so beset with implausibility and inconsistency), yet at the same time wishes to do so."[11]

Why is *Pretty Woman* such a bad film for women? Isn't it just a harmless tale of a poor working girl saved from a life of drudgery by a rich and aristocratic man? In this Pygmalion tale man remakes woman and, in doing so, remakes himself. It is in this conceit—that a poor hooker can "save" a rich but soulless businessman—that the postfeminist emphasis surfaces: "He asks what happens to the prince after he saves Viv's bacon. 'She rescues him right back!' chirps the happy ex-hooker brightly. Viv's rejoinder is the summary example of how *Pretty Woman* veils its exploitative agenda with fashionably feminist leftoid blather."[12] This assumed mutuality between the rich man and the prostitute undercuts and avoids the power relations inherent in the situation of prostitute and john, implicitly equating corporate coldness with prostitution: "*Pretty Woman*'s recommendations on mutual 'rescue' are crucial to its devious work of disavowal. Despite Viv's pretty concluding speech, the film implies that Edward needs little rescue from his circumstances—certainly not from his megabucks—only to become a trifle humanized by Viv's bawdy vitality and the 'special' qualities he discerns in her but never fully articulates."[13]

The class politics of this film are also thoroughly degrading, as the rich man watches the woman perform her working-class ways. The simple but knowing native woman eats with her hands; she is like an animal. But, of course, she is a diamond in the rough, ready to be revealed as such by her knight in shining armor.

Pretty Woman presents an ideology that encourages women to humanize basically good but unfeeling men, men whose emotional coldness is itself a result of their own neglectful fathers. Again, this presents a retro version of feminism, reducing real changes in social relations to the need to teach men to feel and to cry.

In Julia Roberts's next film, *Sleeping with the Enemy*, the answer to wife battering is to pretend you have died, retreat to a gorgeous old mansion in a perfect small town, find the new and sensitive man of your dreams, and live happily ever after. Instances of battering are constructed as the sick acts of lunatic and obsessive men, rather than the everyday practice of everyday men. Jane Caputi argues that *Pretty Woman* and *Sleeping with the Enemy* are not the diametrically opposed films they seem to be, but actually appear "as representing two phases of *one* relationship." The rich rescuer and the abusive husband share many of the same traits, and their control over the women remains based on male power: "In short, these are men defined by their power in the world, epitomized by their power over their lovers."[14]

Presumed Innocent (Figure 16) takes the postfeminist genre to its natural conclusion: "This is yet another plot, like *Fatal Attraction*, about disturbed, sexy ladies who drive decent men crazy. Here another (sterile) blond barges in on a happy family and bewitches a heretofore devoted, responsible husband/father."[15] No longer satisfied with the standard virgin/whore dichotomy played out to such effect

Figure 16. A bad working woman and an even worse wife plague innocent family man Rusty Sabich in *Presumed Innocent*. (Warner Brothers, 1990; photos courtesy of Museum of Modern Art Film Stills Archive)

in *Fatal Attraction*, no longer appeased by the good woman/ bad woman dualism, popular culture now constructs a world where there are no good women, only good men. In a twist on the *Fatal Attraction* theme, *Presumed Innocent* not only makes the sexual, working woman evil incarnate, but constructs the frustrated housewife as warped killer, driven by jealousy to murder her husband's lover: hardworking, white-collar dolts become the fall guys for ambitious, demanding women.

The popularity of David Lynch among the young and restless generation should not be overlooked in a discussion of postfeminism. Lynch has the uniquely postmodern knack of taking that which is, after all, an old story (the virgin/whore; women's pleasure at their own brutalization; the violence at the heart of maternal love) and presenting it as radical new fare for the hip and cynical girl-about-town. Laura Palmer's smitten psychiatrist suggests to the befuddled sheriff in the television series *Twin Peaks* that prom-queen-cum-porn-pervert Laura really wanted to be killed.

The Hand That Rocks the Cradle (Figure 17) presents us with the newest killer woman: the killer nanny as the logical backlash extension of *Fatal Attraction*. Like *Presumed Innocent*, this film involves two errant women. The bad woman here is not the typical working woman, and she is not even in any explicit sense "bad." Rather, the bad woman is the woman who does not take care of her children full time. The message here is twofold: for the nanny it is that thwarted motherhood drives women to madness and evil (evil as in barrenness); for the mom it is that she should take care of her own children and not attempt to work at all (remember, she wanted to build a greenhouse and that is why she needed a nanny). The symbolism here is striking: the mother's fecundity must be channeled

Figure 17.   The film: *The Hand That Rocks the Cradle*. The message: watch your kids day and night or the evil nanny will do it for you. (Buena Vista, 1991; photo courtesy of Photofest)

toward her family, not toward the external world (the greenhouse). Significantly, the greenhouse itself becomes a site of violence, the place where a friend is killed and where the retarded man is set up by the bad nanny as the fall guy for her nefarious deeds.

Strong women of 1980s and 1990s films are shown as legitimately strong through their maternal identification. In *Aliens* tough-lady Ripley (Sigourney Weaver) saves the day, but only after her maternal feelings are awakened and she moves to protect her pseudodaughter Newt from the bad and evil mother monster; the battle of liberation becomes a battle between two mothers. In *Terminator 2*, the muscular mother-warrior must be saved by Arnold the Terminator not because of her own worth but because she carries the savior of the future in her womb: she is literally the mother of the future, rather than the future itself (Figure 18).

Figure 18.   Mother as warrior, warrior as mother in *Aliens* and *Terminator 2: Judgment Day*. (Twentieth Century Fox, 1986, and Tri-Star, 1991; photos courtesy of Photofest and Museum of Modern Art Film Stills Archive)

The list goes on: In the hit *Basic Instinct*, killer lesbians and bisexuals torment weak cops who are brought under their spell and as a result commit rape and murder; women are killers and seductresses, ruining decent but vulnerable men and fathers. In *Poison Ivy*, a young girl's desire for home and family leads her to become a seductress/killer, preying on a weak father and desirous daughter alike until her own death saves the remnants of the nuclear family. The psychotic nurse of Stephen King's *Misery* presents even the classical nurturing woman as a sex-starved psycho, literally holding a man hostage to her tormented fantasies.

Television participates in the backlash as well, although the range of options presented on mainstream television is often greater than that of mainstream film. For all the revisionism and conservatism of contemporary television, we have witnessed several major "women's" programs in the 1980s and early 1990s: *Cagney and Lacey, Murphy Brown, Kate and Allie, Designing Women, Roseanne.* In addition, substantive women characters have emerged on shows such as *Cheers, LA Law,* and the nighttime soaps *Dynasty* and *Dallas.* In fact, given the argument in chapter 3 about gender and genre, it is possible that the growth of prime-time shows following the episodic, inconclusive, multiple-story format of daytime soap operas could provide increased opportunities for a "female gaze" to emerge.

Nevertheless, we do find a trend in television programs similar to that in films of the period—representations that have the veneer of feminism but are actually encoding reactionary ideas about women and women's lives. For example, one of the zeitgeist series of the late 1980s, *thirtysomething*, presented itself as a sophisticated show about today's families and modern life. But once this surface liberalism was scratched, a traditional rendering of women emerged. The "good" woman was, once again, the stay-at-home mother. The career women were stereotypically portrayed as desperate for a man, lonely, often bitter. The men were "relational" new men, yet the social relations of gendered life were little altered; the women, more often than not, were the ones who wrestled with the work/family dilemmas.

The sexual flirtation and banter of popular shows such as *Cheers, Moonlighting,* and *Who's the Boss* seem innocent enough, but in many ways they create narratives in which educated, accomplished women get their comeuppance and are "put in their place" by their working-class counterparts. *Who's the Boss* and *Moonlighting* are programs that offer opportunities for progressive social commentary on the changing nature of work and gender relations. Both shows depict women as bosses and, in one (*Who's the Boss*)

the man performs typical "female" labor. Yet more often
than not, these working women—like the female executive in *Working Girl*—are uptight, rigid, and repressed, and
therefore in need of "thawing" by these more "earthy" men.

In addition, portrayals of women in television seem to
be getting worse over these years. We have moved from
the woman-centered narratives of female attachment in
Cagney and Lacey to the embarrassing portrayal of the
recently divorced public defender Rosie O'Neill, who is
alone, lonely, without a community, eating pizza and
drinking champagne by herself, and talking aimlessly to
her psychiatrist. Elsewhere we meet insipid male teenagers
waiting to score sexually with the nubile teenage girls of
suburbia, or the valiant fireman father trying to take care
of the kids after the mother has precipitously been killed
off. *Uncle Buck, Who's the Boss, Major Dad, Coach, Hunter,
Matlock, Wonder Years, Dear John, The Fanelli Boys, Jake
and the Fatman, The Young Riders*—it becomes obvious:
fathers have returned with a vengeance (witness the amaz-
ing popularity of *The Cosby Show*) but "mothers, in case
you hadn't noticed, are biting the dust in prime-time
comedies. Lately, there has been a weird sort of postfeminist backlash in television's depiction of the American
family, and the message is hardly subliminal: if Mom's not
going to stick around in the kitchen, then—poof—let's
dump her."[16] We have shifted from the golden days of the
1970s (*Mary Tyler Moore, Rhoda, Maude*) to what I call the
paradigm of the Great Disappearing Mother. Of prime-time
shows in the 1991–92 season, only twelve or so include central female characters, and most of these are in half-hour
sitcom formats. Although most single parents are women,
if one only watched television one would think that lots
of men are bravely raising their kids alone. This strange

phenomenon makes Quayle's attack on *Murphy Brown* even more troubling.

Advertisements were no exception to this backlash mood, as images of New Traditionalists (the *Good House-keeping* advertising campaign) and the "little girl" waif model à la Kate Moss vied for public attention. Women were depicted as pouting blonde bombshells 1950s-style for Guess brand jeans, or as corporate executives who wore sexy lingerie and became "real women" after five o'clock.

The intersection between this backlash postfeminism and academic adoption of continental theory is located in one particular characteristic: both varieties of postfeminism share a distorted and revisionist (in the worst sense) history of feminism, signaling the end of a trend even though we have hardly achieved its aims in the first place. The premature declaration of a social movement's demise is no news to anyone familiar with the always shifting sentiments of American popular wisdom (as mediated by popular culture). However, like the declaration that the end of the 1960s signaled the end of social activism, this claim is both wrong and ideologically suspect.

Tellingly, both versions of postfeminism put into question the possibility for any sense of a unity of women, of sisterhood. By claiming a generational dislocation, popular postfeminism distances us forever from "those women" of the 1960s and proclaims the irrelevance of feminism for the hip but overwrought generation of late capitalist yuppies. Academic poststructuralist postfeminism similarly denies the possibility of sisterhood, not through a generational schism but rather through a denial of the category of "woman" altogether. For postmodern postfeminists, feminism was doomed from the start by its allegiance to master narratives (for example, patriarchy) and by its reputed denial of difference in favor of a naive and utopian vision of empowered sisterhood. Luckily postmodernism has come in the nick of time to rescue wayward women from the perils of identification and self-recognition.

Granted, as feminist culture and theory have flourished and developed, they *have* undergone significant intellectual shifts from the early 1970s to the late 1980s that could allow us to speak of a generation of writers and thinkers who have moved past the basic tenets of feminist thought and integrated these with a highly sophisticated understanding of the intellectual currents of postmodernity. Yet my suspicions remain. Judith Stacey's essay "Sexism by a Subtler Name? Postindustrial Conditions and Postfeminist Consciousness in Silicon Valley" claims to "view the term [*postfeminist*] as analogous to 'postrevolutionary' . . . not to indicate the death of the women's movement but to describe the simultaneous incorporation, revision, and depoliticization of many of the central goals of 'second-wave' feminism."[17] For Stacey, postfeminism is not the same as antifeminism; instead postfeminism entails an often unconscious internalization of certain basic feminist goals, with an accompanying depoliticization and individualization of them. Postfeminism is understood as a series of strategies to negotiate the treacherous waters of postindustrial society and its concomitant challenges to traditional family structures, themselves altered fundamentally by second-wave feminism.

Responding to Stacey's essay, Rayna Rapp asks, "Is the legacy of second-wave feminism postfeminism?" First, she develops Stacey's argument by maintaining that the "depoliticization often takes the form of the reduction of feminist *social* goals to individual 'lifestyles.'"[18] She notes as well, quite rightly, that the debates surrounding the term *feminism* were also carried out by first-wave feminists, in the 1920s, who also proclaimed their movement both over and victorious. Finally, in shifting her attention away from Silicon Valley and toward union women in New York City, Rapp argues that the term itself must be located more specifically—that for many women, too busy still struggling over what feminism can bring to them, the designation "post" has no salience whatsoever.

Questions inevitably arise: Is postfeminism really any different from simple backlash? Is it only a trendy code-word for speaking of that which we know to exist: an attack on feminism and women's rights that has been supported and bolstered by eight years of Ronald Reagan and four of George Bush? It seems to me that postfeminism is more problematic than simple backlash, although it clearly includes that. It is more dangerous precisely because it contains elements of clear and explicit antifeminism (for example, the New Right, the Moral Majority, antichoice activism, antigay referenda and initiatives) as well as elements seemingly cognizant and respectful of feminism yet undercutting it with a rewriting of its history and a declaration of its obsolescence for contemporary society. The use of the term *postfeminism* by social theorists such as Stacey feeds into this occlusion.

We also need to place this backlash in a historical context. The backlash of the late 1980s and early 1990s is similar in many ways to the backlash of the late 1940s and 1950s, but differs from it in important aspects. Both eras were responding to serious social transformations. The 1940s experienced a huge influx of women into the labor market during World War II and their desire to stay in that labor force after the war had ended. Many 1940s films were filled with tough working women, independent women, and women who were self-defined. After the war—really during the tail end of it—backlash images began to emerge and working women were vilified, made into monsters who destroyed their children and caused their husbands to run off with other women, and summarily punished for their deviant ways. Newly invigorated images of motherhood filled the screens, women's magazines, and the television images of the 1950s (*Father Knows Best, Donna Reed Show, Leave It to Beaver,* and so on). *I Love Lucy* is significant as an ongoing narrative of a homebound woman always struggling to escape. Most of the show's humor derives from Lucy's desire to move out of the four walls of her apartment and into the world that Ricky inhabits. This attempt is always thwarted by Ricky, who takes Lucy's already doomed efforts in stride as he securely puts her back in her place.

The recent backlash is somewhat different, however. Whereas the backlash in the late 1940s and 1950s carried an explicit message—get out of the workforce and into the kitchen—this time the backlash is couched in the language of liberation, made to seem trendy, even mildly feminist, as in the film *Working Girl.* In addition, this backlash is more clearly antifeminist: it responds directly to the women's movement and often pits one woman against another (*Fatal Attraction, Working Girl, The Hand That Rocks the Cradle*). This backlash is different because it has to *push* motherhood; it must *sell* motherhood and domesticity after those ideologies have already been so soundly critiqued by feminists (unlike in the late 1940s). Furthermore, this backlash contains real violence, as evidenced by the vehemence with which film audiences urge the deaths of femme fatales.

The current period is thus not one of *simple* backlash (such as that of the late 1940s and 1950s) but is characterized by a rewriting of the women's movement to define our era as postfeminist, creating an image of a movement both victorious (the myth that we have achieved equality) and failed (look what feminism got you: double duty, burn-out, and the explosion of your biological clock).

These media images did not, of course, arise in a vacuum. They emerged in a historical period marked by the rise of the New Right and by the governments of Reagan and Bush. These years have seen a growth in antichoice activism (to the point of terrorism and murder), cutbacks on civil rights and equal opportunity legislation of all kinds, and an epidemic of violence against women. The backlash was supported and perpetuated by a government and presidency that spoke to the assembled throngs at the annual Right-to-Life demonstration in Washington, D.C., but maintained a stony silence toward the millions of women who are battered, raped, denied accessible and affordable child care, and paid consistently less than are men. It is disturbing that we see numerous films in which women are depicted as crazed killers when women are more likely to be terrorized by men: the sad irony of *Fatal Attraction*, and the rash of news stories that emerged confirming the "reality" of killer ex-girlfriends, is that it is women not men who are most likely to be hurt at the hands of an ex-lover or ex-spouse.

It is in this climate that we witness the popularity of both *Fatal Attraction* and *Pretty Woman*. These movies are indeed two sides of the same coin: the coin of male control over women's lives, the equation of work for women with death and prostitution. One of the classic ways Hollywood tells a woman to get back in the kitchen and obey her master is by punishing her for wayward behavior. Hollywood films include countless examples of single women, working women, women who are not fulfilled as wives and mothers, sexually active women, and just plain feisty women being summarily killed, humiliated, or simply beaten down. Hollywood has always maintained its support of oppressive social roles for women by refusing to acknowledge that women are both sexual beings and potential parents at the same time.

It is important to recognize that the backlash sentiment has never been so strong. For those of us who teach feminism as a living, breathing, very much alive theory and practice, we experience ourselves as both anachronistic (once again "those shrill women") and frustrated by the reluctance of our female students to "declare" themselves. If identifying oneself as a feminist carried a certain daring and rebellious cachet in the early 1970s, in the early 1990s it is looked on with either a nasty suspicion or (worse, I think) a blasé and tired indifference. As feminism increasingly finds its home in the relative safety of the academy, it becomes somewhat acceptable to be a feminist scholar, but not to be a feminist (as in activist).

Is it not premature to declare a social movement/social theory over when it has yet to achieve even a modicum of egalitarian goals? How can we possibly speak of "postfeminism" when a woman is still raped or beaten every twenty seconds? When women earn roughly half of what men do? When decisions about our bodies are decided by courts and legislatures that are filled with male voices? When the inclusion of women into the academic curriculum is still a piecemeal and embattled process? When fetal rights (really male rights) still assert themselves over the rights of women? When *feminist* is still a dirty word, designed to deny self-determination, power, and legitimacy?

This is not to say that backlash images are the only images—bold shows like *Roseanne* and the growth of alternative feminist film give hope in these trying times. But the thematic and structural overlaps in these various discourses do produce "commonsense" thinking that proves hard to contest. For example, how often do we all speak of the need to "juggle" work and family? How often do we hear a news show that laments the "costs" of feminism and the loneliness of the single woman? These ideologies have seeped into our collective consciousness and have come to appear as truth to many of us. They have emerged not only in the utterances of the popular pundits, but in the narratives of familial life in *thirtysomething* and the cautionary stories of angry and violent women betrayed by their biological clocks and, most dangerously, betrayed by a feminism that "promised it all." What is betrayed, in these backlash discourses, is both the gains women have made in changing our social world and the struggles we must continue to wage.

6

Material Girls
Toward a Feminist Cultural Theory

In the course of this book, several questions and concerns have been posed or implied. In some ways, the most obvious question regards the relationship between the two positions roughly sketched in the first chapter. Are the "images" and "signification" perspectives so dissimilar? Although there are fundamental differences between the two, both theoretically and methodologically, there are some equally fundamental shared assumptions and analytic practices. Most important, perhaps, is the issue that crops up in most debates on cultural criticism and that presents the major stumbling block in the search for a truly critical cultural theory—that is, the question of social relations. For both image and signification theorists, the problem of social relations—and all that implies about social context, history, and politics—is noticeably absent in all but a few of the more recent ethnographic and audience-based studies.

Although the move to close textual analysis, influenced by semiotics and narrative theory, has been heralded as something new and radical, it remains dubiously linked to the content studies of earlier generations. For the "image" theorist engaged in content analysis and the "signification" theorist engaged in textual analysis alike, the media text becomes reified: the text becomes the beginning and end of cultural critique, the subject and the object of analysis. In fact, the more mainstream feminist communications researchers often paid more attention to social context, albeit in a limited way. Effects studies, problematic as they are, at least address themselves to a question central to any critical cultural analysis: What are the "effects" of the media on people's lives? Clearly, theorizing the media in terms of effects assumes a one-way flow model of indoctrination that has rightly been criticized in recent years, particularly by critics on the left. Nevertheless, much of early feminist work (for example, Tuchman) was explicitly concerned with the social effects of media images; this cannot always be said of the signification research.

In addition, both "sides" avoid the specificity of the audience member (exceptions again include the more recent feminist work on audience). In the psychoanalytic work, she is either presumed male or, more generally, *positioned* by the workings of the text and the generic psychic patterns of the implied spectator. Similarly, the "images" work either ignores the viewer altogether (for example, in content studies) or renders her generic and anonymous in the haze of numbers that pour forth from the effects studies. In either case, the specificity of the female viewer in terms of race, class, sexual preference, national identity, and so on, is overlooked, rendering her either absent or implied by the textual operations.

This evacuation of social relations, shared by both groups of critics, means that the historicity of media images is denied or, at the very least, avoided. Cultural criticism, in both these forms of analysis, prefers to position itself as an island, a world unto itself. The social context of the production, distribution, and reception of certain images is thus largely ignored or left to more journalistic and popular interventions (such as the books by Haskell and Rosen).

For all these similarities, feminist signification theorists *have* added greatly to the body of knowledge within cultural analysis. The concern with the position of women in narratives and in particular genres, the attention to the ways in which patriarchy not only structures content but informs our very "way of seeing," and the emphasis on the "constructedness" and "productiveness" of images have provided the tools for numerous revealing and deconstructive analyses of media texts. Nonetheless, serious problems remain.

The most fundamental problem stems from the issues raised earlier concerning the absence of social relations. One would expect feminist theories of representation to articulate a decidedly woman-centered framework for the analysis of cultural phenomena. That is, one would expect an analysis that *begins* from the premises of feminist theory and analysis. Yet this discourse, drawing as it does so fundamentally from Lacanian psychoanalysis and linguistic and semiotic models, often seems more engaged with detailing the internal system of "filmic texts" than with advancing the feminist project:

> When psychoanalysis is applied to film, the potential for theorizing alternative readings or interpretations within any given text is inhibited by a denial of viewing *contexts*: no place is allowed for shifts in textual meaning related to shifts in viewing situation. As a result, varying social groups . . . are readily assumed to have the same viewing experience. At the same time, audiences of differing historical periods and circumstances . . . are all assumed to

be positioned by, and therefore to interpret, a text in the same manner.[1]

In struggling to make apparent the difference between "women" as real historical beings and "woman" as she is constructed in and through the male gaze, the former view is often lost, or at least held in perpetual suspension. For even though many of these feminist signification theorists claim to make the distinction between "woman" and "women" and purport that they are interested in delineating the relationship between the two, they never seem to get to women qua women. For if there is not a "real" or "true" image of "woman," there are, after all is said and done, flesh and blood women out there in the world, a point that feminist *social* theory has continually reiterated in its stress on experience and the attempt to theorize from a feminist *standpoint*.[2]

Why are women absent in so much of feminist cultural criticism? The reasons are varied. Clearly, the absence of women in the discourse of feminist film criticism, for example, partly involves the formalistic tendencies of most of that work. Talking about women would entail a social and historical analysis that breaks away from the formal and ahistoric categories of most current discourse on the "signifying process." The notion of "signifying system," especially in film theory, tends to become a self-enclosed, overly formalistic mechanism for detaching the celluloid from the social. The only historicity we can find is the historicity of the film practice itself, stripped away from the social practices from which it emerged. As Michele Barrett notes, "In so far as a knowledge of real social relations is denied, it must follow that discourse itself must be the site of struggle. We do not seek a cultural revolution; we seek a revolution in discourse."[3]

Most important, women are absent because all too often politics (and therefore history) are absent. If the discourse of feminist film criticism is embedded within a larger discourse that we may call poststructuralism, then we may do well to question the politics of poststructuralism. But let us return to the referent, and consider this question of poststructuralism and politics through the eyes of women, real women, women who have historically been denied their subjectivity. We may wonder about what a politics that posits no referent has to offer women. It seems both dangerous and unwise for women to accept the concept of the loss of the subject, the demise of the referent. It is easy to wave a fond farewell to the subject when one is assured that, after all, one *is* the subject (white, middle-class men, for example); as Modleski so succinctly puts it, "The death of the social is another of phallocentrism's masks, likewise authorising the 'end of woman' without consulting her."[4] For women, whose very existence has been defined ideologically in terms of our *lack* of that subjectivity, the issue remains much more complex:

> The viewing subject has to a certain extent displaced the social audience—both as object of knowledge and site of social transformation. Heterogeneity has been invoked as a conceptual tool to put the subject in crisis—the viewing subject. . . . But one gains the impression that the audience . . . has assumed an unquestioned homogeneity in part guaranteed by unanimous agreement that the subject must be put in crisis, decentered, thus ironically ensuring a very safe, central and functional place to the concept of the subject as an imaginary category. An assault on the ideological concept of audience . . . has resulted in a retreat from the social.[5]

In an ironic way, signification theorists—with all their emphasis on heterogeneity and plurality, excess and transgression—seem to posit an almost Weberian ideal type in referring to the spectator. Real social differences, of class, of race, of sexual preference, of ethnicity, are erased in the ideal type categories of masculine and feminine subject positions and constructions of desire, "as if all that men and women brought with them to a movie theater, or what they regressed to, as the Lacanian model would have it, were their earliest psychological fears and desires."[6]

While "women" are avoided, femininity and the feminine are constantly evoked. Yet femininity is not interchangeable with women, although it is clearly a part of the construction of a female identity. Again, evoking "femininity" as an all-encompassing, transhistorical quality to describe the condition of women under patriarchy avoids a more nuanced and detailed discussion of different femininities and other forms of female behavior that perhaps do not neatly fit into that category. Thus, once again, the specificity of the reader/spectator, a specificity that is *theorized* and stressed in the discourse of signification theorists, is effectively denied in their critical practice:

> Other criticisms of the semiotic/psychoanalytic problematic focussed on its abstraction and over-generalization. Psychoanalysis seemed to mandate and perpetuate a treatment of spectatorship that was ahistorical. The urge to move beyond generalities, or to test them against particular instances, manifested itself both in a renewed search for historical specificity in modes of spectatorship . . . and in approaches inspired by work in British cultural studies.[7]

The reliance on a psychoanalytic framework for analysis (mostly Lacanian these days) relegates even the complex *social* practice of representation to a few grand metaphors. It is a problem for women when "Oedipal" becomes the dominant metaphor through which our relationship to representation is defined. The production of difference does occur in representation, but to locate it so narrowly within timeless psychic processes is to avoid both the social construction of difference and the heterogeneity of differences present in any given audience. The use of the Oedipal metaphor as a grand signifier of the workings of representation, particularly as it relates to narrative (see, for example, de Lauretis, for whom narrative equals desire equals Oedipus), loses sight of the social constructedness of the Oedipal conjuncture itself.

If we have now done away with the mechanistic and degrading concept of "false consciousness," we must present some other way of explaining our investment in ideologies and practices that serve only to reinforce our own oppression. Often psychoanalysis is offered as an explanation for the seemingly intractable commitment to relationships and modes of behavior that are clearly "bad" for us. Modleski justifies the use of psychoanalytic concepts in her analysis of various forms of romance by noting that psychoanalysis "helps explain, for example, why the sales of Harlequin Romances have not simply remained steady in recent years, but have steadily increased along with the growth of feminism. Only by taking psychoanalytic insights into account . . . can we begin to explain why women are still requiring what Jameson calls the 'symbolic satisfactions' of the texts instead of looking for 'real' satisfactions."[8] The "goal" here is no different from that of earlier, orthodox marxist cultural critics: to find out why people are duped, why they are satisfied with fantasy at the expense of pursuing a new reality. This in itself is problematic, as it assumes a solely compensatory function for mass culture. Even more problematic is Modleski's assumption that the cultural critic, when faced with her own bewilderment over the dubious pleasures of mass culture, "must" take psychoanalytic insights into account. Psychoanalysis is placed as the "truth" that underlies the surface realities of women's lives; the feminist critic can now "explain" false consciousness with the "truth" of psychoanalysis in much the same way that an earlier marxist critic could "explain" it with the "truth" of historical materialism.

Yet psychoanalysis (or historical materialism, for that matter) is not the only way to explain enduring contradictions and the seemingly self-defeating investments so many of us make in structures of oppression. Indeed, using Modleski's own example, one might want to "explain" this phenomenon precisely in terms of the changing social conditions fostered by feminism, thus placing these "symbolic satisfactions" in a historical and social context. For example, we may want to understand the pleasure so many women expressed at the recent film *Pretty Woman* not by the deep, inherent desire to be rescued by a man but rather by a social context of backlash in which women experience an abiding cynicism about the possibilities of heterosexual mutuality. I remain unconvinced of the *necessity* of psychoanalytic constructs as an explanatory model, although I do not, of course, rule it out as one possible method among many.

An examination of the work of the signification theorists also poses the question of accessibility, a question conveniently overlooked in most cutting-edge discourse but one that feminists clearly cannot afford to ignore. In the rush to keep up with the newest thinking, cultural critics find their writing is inaccessible to even the most forward thinking of the general public. Cultural criticism, more than any other method of critical thought, must struggle to make itself known. For if the image so often mystifies and degrades us, our criticism of that same image should not—must not—participate in further mystification. If the point of cultural analysis is to demystify, to make available alternative and oppositional readings of cultural objects that often appear transparent to us in their simplicity and innocuousness, then it hardly serves our purpose to regale ourselves with endless speculations on the floating signifier and musings on the impossibility of reading. If we want to reveal the ideological agendas that are often inscribed in a cultural text, then to use language and analysis that are deeply inaccessible and severely laden with jargon only further removes that cultural text from the comprehension and control of those consumers for whom the agendas are intended.

The issue of accessibility is a particularly troubling one for feminists. If part of the feminist project has always been to ground theory and knowledge in the real experiences of women and to avoid the kind of abstractions that have historically been used to exclude the female voice, then a theoretical practice that is weighted with jargon occupies a suspicious place within feminist theory.

This inaccessibility is a result not only of the increasing academicism of feminist cultural critique, but also of a certain narrowing of focus. This contraction has occurred on two levels. On the one hand, it reflects the increasingly text-based studies and the consequent absence of a broader context, resulting in the esoteric reductionism that Michele Barrett cautions against: "We must avoid making the text itself our only basis for analysis. . . . To restrict our analysis solely to the text itself is to turn the *object* of analysis into its own means of explanation. . . . To reduce the problem solely to the text is a form of reductionism as unprofitable as reducing it to the mechanical expression of economic relations."[9] On the other hand, the narrow focus also is connected to the tentative microanalyses provoked by the poststructuralist critique of grand theory and master narrative. Although this book is not the place to wrestle with that whole question, it must be said that poststructuralist discourse has made us wary of drawing links and positing more general claims about, for example, women and representation *across* different media, lest we be accused of constructing an oppressive totalizing theory. Although we do need to be cautious of reinserting the dominant narratives into our analyses, we must make connections between our particular cultural analyses and the larger social fabric if we are to be political in our work. To paraphrase Marx: up until now, cultural critics have been content to read a text; the point, however, is to write a new one.

If these two positions (the image perspective and the signification approach), though interesting and illuminating to a great extent, still remain inadequate to the project of developing a feminist cultural theory or standpoint, then what may be suggested in their stead? My criticisms of both the image and the signification theorists suggest a direction, although an admittedly unmapped one. It is important to note here that the direction I am suggesting—a feminist cultural studies—is not unique. Indeed, as the last few chapters have indicated, many theorists, perhaps disenchanted with the psychoanalytic framework, perhaps prodded by the postmodern merging of image and reality, have moved in this intertextual, contextual direction.

Clearly, I do not believe a return to the quantitative and descriptive approach of the early researchers on images of women in the mass media is a valuable way to address the problems raised by my critique of the signification theorists. Yet I also do not believe that the latter position needs simply to be deepened, or even politicized, for my criticisms to become moot. What we need is a feminist cultural criticism that has the theoretical sophistication of signification theory—a framework deeply critical of the dominant representations of women—but is informed by a committed feminist praxis.

If feminism is both a way of understanding the world and a politics, then does it not follow that theories of culture, while borrowing from a variety of perspectives, should develop fundamentally from *feminism*, particularly in terms of methodology? This is not to say that feminist cultural theorists should not engage with semiotics or other methods of decoding cultural objects, but that these approaches should be used to enhance *feminist* cultural theorizing, rather than the other way around. In other words, by arguing for a feminist *cultural* theory (not necessarily in opposition to a feminist film theory, or a feminist analysis of advertising, or a feminist theory of television, but perhaps inclusive of them), I am suggesting that feminism has the analytic power to act as a significant decoder of the cultural products of late capitalist patriarchy. Studies across different media are thus of the utmost importance: "While paintings, pin-ups, news photographs, fashion and photographic images vary considerably in the ways in which they are produced and consumed, they overlap and intersect in their representations of femininity and female sexuality. It therefore makes sense to look at the ways in which the feminine image is constructed across a range of differing cultural practices."[10] In fact, I am going even further by suggesting that women's unique position vis-à-vis mass culture (woman as both subject and object, as the one defined by that which she is not—"man"—as the body through which difference is produced) renders feminism *as a standpoint* privileged access to the arduous process of demystification and subversive interpretation.

I am calling for not simply a new focus, but rather a new conceptualization of what the project of feminist cultural criticism can be. The research emanating from the Centre for Contemporary Cultural Studies of the University of Birmingham[11] remains helpful in the development of a view of cultural studies that avoids the rigid and limiting orthodoxics of various reflection hypotheses as well as struggles against the dangers of a politically empty poststructuralism.

First, however, it is necessary to take a brief detour into ideology, as it has been noticeably absent from this book thus far. This is no simple oversight; the reasons for its absence here are quite revealing of the state of feminist cultural studies. I can offer only a somewhat paradoxical explanation for this absence of ideology. On the one hand, the recognition of the ideological nature of images and the mass media in general is by now accepted among critical cultural theorists. The "role" that the media play in producing and reproducing the terms of dominant (patriarchal, capitalist) culture has been thoroughly acknowledged and assimilated into the analytic frameworks of most theorists who are vaguely on the left, including most of the theorists discussed earlier. In a sense, "ideology critique" can be found across the broad spectrum of feminist criticism. For example, both E. Ann Kaplan and Rosalind Coward include ideological critique within a psychoanalytic framework, and Judith Williamson combines it with semiotics. Annette Kuhn has explicitly argued that feminist textual analysis is, by its very nature, ideological criticism:

> A textual analysis whose objective is to uncover this process of signification will, according to this argument, also—as an intended or unintended consequence—uncover the textual operations of ideology. That is to say, such an approach can constitute what has been termed an ideological analysis. Structuralist and semiotic approaches to textual analy-

sis which take up this notion of ideology are founded, therefore, on the twofold assumption that part of the work of
ideology is to conceal its own operation, and that this operation can have its own independent effects with cultural
productions. . . . Feminist textual analysis then, by exam-
ining ways in which films embody and construct patriarchal ideology, by undercutting these ideological operations
and by offering alternative ways of looking at films, may
be regarded as an intervention within ideology.[12]

If ideology is everywhere, then it is also, paradoxically,
nowhere. The debates over the meaning of the term *ideology*, prompted in part by Althusser but continued and
heightened by Michel Foucault and the "language turn"
of poststructuralism, have rendered the word so problematic that the term *ideology* has, to a great extent, been
replaced by *discourse*. Even when ideology *is* retained, its
relationship to its marxist heritage (ideology as partial
knowledge, as mystifying, as the opposite of that which is
true and material) is often lost or glossed over.

This wariness toward ideology is, in part, a healthy
response to the denigrating use of the term to describe the
compensatory pleasures of mass culture (for example, false
consciousness). The pleasures of popular culture can no
longer be designated simply as the false consciousness of
the masses held under the sway of capitalist ideology. Yet
the post-Althusserian battle cry—"the materiality of ideology"—disengages both terms from any substantive
meaning and can result in a glib celebration of "the popular" that obscures the notion of ideology as dominant and
dominating *power*: "What seems to be happening here, and
it is a worrying trend, is that by celebrating on the one
hand an active audience for popular forms and on the other
those popular forms which the audience 'enjoy,' we appear
to be throwing the whole enterprise of cultural critique

out of the window."[13] In sum, while there are feminists who continue to produce what might be called marxist-feminist cultural criticism, such as Michele Barrett and Judith Williamson, one is hard-pressed to cite many feminists who are exclusively working within what used to be called "ideology critique." It often appears as if the psychoanalytic (or semiotic, or structuralist) framework comes first, and the analysis of ideology, such as it is, must fit into this paradigm.

One of the essential components of British cultural studies, therefore, is its refusal to do away with ideology as an important and compelling analytic category. In this regard, it maintains a focus on the circuits of power and domination that are vital to a feminist and marxist critique of popular culture. British cultural theory represents a body of work that has been characterized by its persistent intervention upon marxism and its struggle to develop a conceptualization of "culture" that does not succumb to either economic reductionism or to a vague, all-inclusive idealism. This attempt at reconceptualization has necessitated an interaction with orthodox marxism as well as the marxist traditions embodied in the work of the Frankfurt School, Antonio Gramsci, Althusser, and the whole of what has come to be known as Western marxism. Out of this process of critique and analysis has emerged an ambitious and not unproblematic attempt at synthesis, taking insights culled from a variety of traditions both inside marxism (Marx and Engels, Althusser, Gramsci, Georg Lukács) and outside it (semiotics, Roland Barthes, Lacanian psychoanalysis, film theory, poststructuralism).

In response to both pessimistic Frankfurt School mass culture theory and the direct socialization hypothesis of most early American communications studies, the Birmingham perspective offers a series of arguments, empirical studies, and theoretical conceptualizations that are explicitly antireductionist in method and tone. The search here is for an analysis of popular culture that sees the moments of resistance and containment, the contradictory and dialectical movements of domination and subversion. The field of "culture"—in its more institutionalized forms in the mass media as well as in its less formal, local manifestations—is seen as a highly contested terrain of transformations and mediations. In its continuous rethinking of the marxist project, this interdisciplinary perspective can offer feminists new ways of conceptualizing the relationship between marxism and feminism, the previous discussion of which has produced a dead-end debate on the unhappy marriage of marxism and feminism—an unfortunate metaphor to be sure.

The Birmingham approach to cultural studies thus originally appeared to be the panacea for the twin evils of economistic marxism and esoteric intellectualism, but also seemed especially appropriate to what has since been called the "postmodern condition." It is, however, not without its problems. Although I often saw an intellectual affinity between British marxist cultural theory and feminism in their shared emphasis on "lived experience" and their commitment to releasing the suppressed voices of those typically seen as somehow "outside" culture, nevertheless the emphasis remained resolutely class-based, with "women" or "girls" occasionally grafted onto an already established cultural framework.[14] The insights of feminism were often mentioned but rarely served to transform either the methodology or the choice of cultural objects to be analyzed. Yet the affinity remains.

In simple terms, British cultural theorists look at *people*—a daring thing to do in an intellectual milieu that has boldly declared the end of social relations. More important, this ethnographic impulse is informed by a sustained and developed political sensibility, so that the studies have the richness and vitality that only an engagement with lived experience can produce. It seems deeply contradictory for feminist film theorists (for example) to consistently avoid discussion of *women* while speaking eloquently of the construction of *woman* in and through representation. If it has always been a patriarchal strategy to represent woman as image, as symbol, as metaphor for male desire (as the feminist film critics so thoroughly point out), then it behooves us to do more than reiterate this point (woman as "lack," as "absence," as signifier). Although delineating the workings of patriarchy as it constructs woman as signifier is vital—and a first step toward any critical cultural analysis—it becomes vacant when the relationship between "woman" and "women" is continually held in abeyance.

Ethnographic and audience-based research is likewise not without its own set of problems, however, as mentioned in chapter 4. For example, Ien Ang's study of the nighttime soap opera *Dallas* turns her anonymous female respondents into so many "texts" for her critical analysis. Ang's "informants" (women who responded by letter to a women's magazine advertisement soliciting their feelings about *Dallas*) have no history, no social context, no identity, and as a consequence resemble the statistical outcome of an "effects" study. The resulting analysis of *Dallas* and the meaning it has for women is correspondingly weak; one feels Ang could have come to the same conclusions without the letters.[15] Similarly, David Morley's study *Family Television*, while interesting and often entertaining, fails to provide the more layered and textured analysis that an encounter with "real audiences" should, in principle, do. His conclusions, like Ang's, could have been arrived at through *any* critical perspective.[16] Of course, ethnographic work cannot "guarantee" truth any more than can a purely textual analysis.

Yet other studies, like those of Janice Radway, stand as examples of the possibility of reuniting text and context within a critical feminist perspective. In this regard, an emphasis on some sort of (nonempiricist) empirical research should be part of the project, particularly if one attempts to turn the feminist phrase "the personal is political" into a methodological principle. Methodologically, this approach would entail a move away from the focus on either the isolated text or the aggregate viewer and a move toward an engagement with the lived experience of actual women, an engagement with "material girls." I want to stress that this engagement need not be seen literally, as interviews or ethnographies. Rather, the methods increasingly used by feminist cultural critics are refreshingly eclectic, merging sophisticated textual analyses with social history, genre criticism with object relations, interviews with fan mail. Indeed, these intertextual, contextual critics are redefining what we mean by "audience" and what we mean by "empirical research." Feminist cultural criticism should continue to push these boundaries, while always maintaining a firm commitment to asking fundamentally *feminist* questions of cultural processes.

Radway, one of the writers in the vanguard of feminist cultural methodology, now has suggested a shift toward an ethnographic, collaborative team of researchers who study the leisure practices of a particular heterogeneous community, or what she calls a "leisure world."[17] She recognizes the problems of reception theory and audience studies but insists that we must still move in that direction if we are to produce accounts of the interactions between popular culture and women's consciousness and women's lives:

If we are *not* to begin with reception . . . where should we start? Instead of segmenting a social formation automatically by construing it precisely as a set of audiences for specific media and/or genres, I have been wondering whether it might not be more fruitful to start with the habits and practices of everyday life as they are actively, discontinuously, even contradictorily pieced together by historical subjects as they move nomadically via disparate associations and relations through day-to-day existence. In effect, I have begun to wonder whether our theories do not impress upon us a new object of analysis, one more difficult to analyze because it can't be so easily pinned down— that is, the endlessly shifting, ever-evolving kaleidoscope of daily life, and the way in which the media are integrated and implicated within it.[18]

This is a direction feminist cultural theory must move in, if it is to take seriously its desire to demystify dominant cultural products and to help construct a liberatory and expressive feminist culture.

Notes

Introduction

1. Cathy Schwichtenberg, ed., *The Madonna Connection* (Boulder: Westview Press, 1993).

2. Shelagh Young, "Feminism and the Politics of Power: Whose Gaze Is It Anyway?" in *The Female Gaze: Women as Viewers of Popular Culture*, ed. Lorraine Gamman and Margaret Marshment (London: The Women's Press, 1988), 183–84.

3. Sharon Willis, "Hardware and Hardbodies: What Do Women Really Want? A Reading of *Thelma and Louise*," in *Film Theory Goes to the Movies*, ed. Jim Collins, Hilary Radner, and Ava Preacher Collins (New York: Routledge, 1993), 120.

4. John Robinson, "He Hates It," *Boston Globe*, 14 June 1991, 29.

5. John Leo, "Toxic Feminism on the Big Screen," *U.S. News and World Report*, 10 June 1991, 20.

6. Robinson, "He Hates It," 36.

7. Ibid., 29, 36.

8. Leo, "Toxic Feminism," 20.

9. Few critics have challenged this strange phrase. In a world in which women *are* systematically "bashed" (raped, abandoned, harassed, etc.), it is a sad irony that the term *male-bashing* is the one that has entered cultural discourse.

10. Robert Novak, *"Thelma and Louise,"* *People Weekly*, 10 June 1991, 18.

11. John Simon, "Movie of the Moment," *National Review*, 8 July 1991, 48.

12. Ibid., 50.

13. Diane White, "She Loves It (The Great Debate over Thelma and Louise)," *Boston Globe*, 14 June 1991, 29.

14. Mary Cantwell, "What Were the Women 'Asking' For?" *New York Times*, 13 June 1991, A28.

15. Geena Davis as quoted in Jim Jerome, "Riding Shotgun," *People Weekly*, 24 June 1991, 91.

16. Jay Carr, "Out There," *Boston Globe*, 30 June 1991, B6.

17. Margaret Carlson, "Is This What Feminism Is All About?" *Time*, 24 June 1991, 57.

18. This is in vivid contrast to a feminist film of the early 1980s (Marlene Gorris's *A Question of Silence*) in which a group of unconnected women join together in the murder of an innocuous shopkeeper.

19. Manohla Dargis, "Guns N' Poses," *Village Voice*, 16 July 1991, 22.

20. J. E. Yang and A. Devroy, "Quayle: 'Hollywood Doesn't Get It,'" *Washington Post*, 21 May 1992, A1, A17.

21. Dorothy Rabinowitz, "Politics as Usual in Hollywood," *Wall Street Journal*, 21 September 1992, A10.

22. Elizabeth Kolbert, "'Murphy Brown' Feud: When Art Replaces Life," *New York Times*, 23 September 1992, 21.

23. John Leo, "A Pox on Dan and Murphy," *U.S. News and World Report*, 1 June 1992, 19.

24. Barbara Dafoe Whitehead, "What Is Murphy Brown Saying? For Starters, That Unwed Motherhood Is a Glamorous Option," *Washington Post*, 10 May 1992, C5.

25. Douglas Besharov, "Beyond Murphy Brown," *Washington Post*, 27 June 1992, C3.

26. Ellen Snortland, "'Values' Is Code for 'Dad Is the Boss,'" *Los Angeles Times*, 22 May 1992, B7.

27. Rickie Solinger, "Murphy Brown, at the Pinnacle of Choice," *Los Angeles Times*, 17 May 1992, M5.

28. Dorothy Gilliam, "Quayle-Brown Nonsense Obscures Real Family Issues," *Washington Post*, 23 September 1992, B1.

29. As quoted in Douglas Jehl, "Quayle Deplores Eroding Values; Cites TV Show," *Los Angeles Times*, 20 May 1992, A14.

30. The early and mid-1970s really mark the beginning of a literature on women and representation, coterminous with the growth of the women's movement, as is discussed in the next chapter.

31. This book is limited to theories of visual representation and culture generally, and thus avoids dealing with the enormous literature that makes up the field of feminist literary criticism, which has, to some extent, stood separate from the more general work on women and culture and women and representation. The relationship between this field of literary criticism and feminist theories of visual representation awaits further analysis.

32. Lacanian film studies draw on the work of French psychoanalyst Jacques Lacan, whose writings have come to be central to both literary criticism specifically and cultural theory more generally. Lacan has been appropriated for film theory (feminist and otherwise) because of his emphasis on language and the relationship between signification and subjectivity. He argued that the subject is formed by language, or sign systems, which themselves make the very conditions for identity possible. For a good summary of Lacan in relation to film theory, see Kaja Silverman, *The Subject of Semiotics* (New York: Oxford University Press, 1983).

33. The Frankfurt School refers to the group of left-wing intellectuals grouped around the Institute for Social Research in Frankfurt, Germany, who later emigrated to the United States, mostly before World War II. The Frankfurt School theorists, particularly Theodor Adorno and Max Horkheimer, are central figures in the development of cultural studies. They are known for their belief in the wholly "negative" effects of mass culture, which turns individuals into virtual automatons who passively desire

to consume that which deceives them and then turns them into commodities themselves.

34. Laura Kipnis, "'Refunctioning' Reconsidered: Towards a Left Popular Culture," in *High Theory/Low Culture. Analyzing Popular Television and Film,* ed. Colin MacCabe (New York: St. Martin's Press, 1986), 15.

35. Ibid., 17.

36. Teresa de Lauretis, *Alice Doesn't: Feminism, Semiotics, Cinema* (Bloomington: Indiana University Press, 1984), 15.

37. Ibid.

38. Annette Kuhn, *Women's Pictures: Feminism and Cinema* (London: Routledge and Kegan Paul, 1982), 4.

39. E. Ann Kaplan, "Feminist Criticism and Television," in *Channels of Discourse: Television and Contemporary Criticism,* ed. Robert C. Allen (Chapel Hill: University of North Carolina Press, 1987), 215.

40. The overlap between theory and practice is substantial. Examples of this include the films and theoretical work of Laura Mulvey and Yvonne Rainer and the early work of Mary Kelly (e.g., her "Post-partum Document"), which is both theory and cultural product. In addition, much feminist artistic practice contains within it an explicit critique of the patriarchal construction of images. See particularly the photographers Cindy Sherman and Barbara Kruger.

41. Rosemary Betterton, "Introduction: Feminism, Femininity and Representation," in *Looking On: Images of Femininity in the Visual Arts and Media,* ed. Rosemary Betterton (London: Pandora Press, 1987), 1–17.

42. De Lauretis, *Alice Doesn't,* 15.

43. Tania Modleski, "Femininity as Mas(s)querade: A Feminist Approach to Mass Culture," in MacCabe, *High Theory/Low Culture,* 37–52.

44. Judith Williamson, "Woman Is an Island: Femininity and Colonization," in *Studies in Entertainment: Critical Approaches to Mass Culture,* ed. Tania Modleski (Bloomington: Indiana University Press, 1986), 99–118.

45. Unfortunately, I am not able to cover here, except in passing, feminist cultural criticism that centers on explicitly feminist representations. This book focuses instead on mass-market, mainstream popular culture and the frameworks developed to analyze and critique these representations.

46. Clearly, I am simplifying and unifying these diverse positions for the sake of expediency. In fact, there are serious differences within the "signification" perspective, differences that often have to do with the extent to which a commitment to a marxist or materialist framework is retained. *Poststructuralism* is a hopelessly inadequate and fragmented term to cover the range of positions. Recently, the term *cine-feminism* has been used to characterize a practice focused on questions of the cinema as a signifying apparatus within which issues of genre, style, and the production of sexual difference figure heavily.

1. From Images of Women to Woman as Image

1. Kuhn, *Women's Pictures*, 75.

2. Gaye Tuchman, "The Newspaper as a Social Movement's Resource," in *Hearth and Home: Images of Women in the Mass Media*, ed. Gaye Tuchman, Arlene Kaplan Daniels, and James Benet (New York: Oxford University Press, 1978), 186–215.

3. Robin Morgan, ed., *Sisterhood Is Powerful: An Anthology of Writings from the Women's Liberation Movement* (New York: Vintage Books / Random House, 1970), 584–85.

4. United States Commission on Civil Rights, *Window Dressing on the Set: Women and Minorities in Television* (Washington, D.C.: U.S. Government Printing Office, 1997).

5. Helen Baehr, "The Impact of Feminism on Media Studies— Just Another Commercial Break?" in *Men's Studies Modified: The Impact of Feminism on the Academic Disciplines*, ed. Dale Spender (New York: Athene Series / Pergamon Press, 1981), 146.

6. Linda Busby, "Sex-Role Research on the Mass Media," *Journal of Communication* 25, no. 4 (autumn 1975): 122.

7. Ibid.

8. Ibid.

9. Gaye Tuchman, "Introduction: The Symbolic Annihilation of Women by the Mass Media," in Tuchman, Daniels, and Benet, *Hearth and Home*, 6.

10. Ibid., 8.

11. George Gerbner, "The Dynamics of Cultural Resistance," in Tuchman, Daniels, and Benet, *Hearth and Home*, 46–50.

12. Tuchman, "The Symbolic Annihilation of Women by the Mass Media," 37.

13. Rosemary Betterton, ed., *Looking On: Images of Femininity in the Visual Arts and Media* (London: Pandora Press, 1987), 20.

14. Leslie H. Steeves, "Feminist Theories and Media Studies," *Critical Studies in Mass Communication* 4, no. 2 (June 1987): 101–2.

15. Mary Ann Doane, Patricia Mellencamp, and Linda Williams, "Feminist Film Criticism: An Introduction," in *Re-Vision: Essays in Feminist Film Criticism*, ed. Mary Ann Doane, Patricia Mellencamp, and Linda Williams (Los Angeles: American Film Institute, 1984), 6.

16. Baehr, "The Impact of Feminism on Media Studies," 148.

17. Griselda Pollock, "What's Wrong with Images of Women?" *Screen* 24 (autumn 1977): 26.

18. Kuhn, *Women's Pictures*, 75.

19. Rosemary Betterton, "How Do Women Look? The Female Nude in the Work of Suzanne Valadon," in Betterton, *Looking On: Images of Femininity in the Visual Arts and Media*, 219.

20. See especially T. E. Perkins, "Rethinking Stereotypes," in *Ideology and Cultural Production*, ed. Michele Barrett et al. (New York: St. Martin's Press, 1979).

21. Ibid., 136–38.

22. Kuhn, *Women's Pictures*, 73.

23. Jackie Byars, *All That Hollywood Allows: Re-reading Gender in 1950s Melodrama* (Chapel Hill: University of North Carolina Press, 1991), 69.

24. Pollock, "What's Wrong with Images of Women?" 26.

25. Kuhn, *Women's Pictures*, 19.

26. Teresa de Lauretis, "Aesthetic and Feminist Theory: Rethinking Women's Cinema," in *Female Spectators: Looking at Film and Television*, ed. E. Deidre Pribram (London: Verso, 1988), 174–75.

2. Visual Pressures

1. Mary Devereaux, "Oppressive Texts, Resisting Readers, and the Gendered Spectator: The New Aesthetics," *Journal of Aesthetics and Art Criticism* 48, no. 4 (fall 1990): 342.

2. John Berger, *Ways of Seeing* (London: British Broadcasting Corporation, and Harmondsworth: Penguin, 1972), 46–47.

3. Ibid., 64.

4. Ibid., 55.

5. Ibid., 46.

6. Mary Ann Doane, *Femmes Fatales: Feminism, Film Theory, Psychoanalysis* (New York: Routledge, 1991), 7.

7. Kaja Silverman, "Dis-Embodying the Female Voice," in Doane, Mellencamp, and Williams, *Re-Vision: Essays in Feminist Film Criticism*, 131.

8. Rosalind Coward, *Female Desires: How They Are Sought, Bought and Packaged* (New York: Grove Press, 1985), 76–77.

9. Gaylyn Studlar, "Masochism, Masquerade, and the Erotic Metamorphoses of Marlene Dietrich," in *Fabrications: Costume and the Female Body*, ed. Jane Gaines and Charlotte Herzog (New York: Routledge, 1990), 230.

10. Laura Mulvey, *Visual and Other Pleasures* (Bloomington: Indiana University Press, 1989), 25.

11. Janice Winship, "Handling Sex," in Betterton, *Looking On: Images of Femininity in the Visual Arts and Media*, 25.

12. Coward, *Female Desires*, 81.

13. De Lauretis, *Alice Doesn't*, 139.

14. Devereaux, "Oppressive Texts, Resisting Readers, and the Gendered Spectator," 337.

15. Ibid., 339.

16. E. Ann Kaplan, *Women and Film: Both Sides of the Camera* (New York: Methuen, 1983), 31.

17. Noel Carroll, "The Image of Women in Film: A Defence of a Paradigm," *Journal of Aesthetics and Art Criticism* 48 (fall 1990): 351.

18. Mulvey, *Visual and Other Pleasures*, 19.

19. Betterton, "How Do Women Look?" 219.

20. Mary Ann Doane, "Woman's Stake: Filming the Female Body," *October* 17 (summer 1981), reprinted in *Feminism and Film Theory*, ed. Constance Penley (New York: Routledge, 1988), 216.

21. Betterton, "How Do Women Look?" 220.

22. Mary Ann Doane, "Film and the Masquerade: Theorizing the Female Spectator," *Screen* 23 (September-October 1982), reprinted in *Issues in Film Criticism*, ed. Patricia Erens (Bloomington: Indiana University Press, 1990), 47.

23. Ibid., 48.

24. Ibid., 54.

25. Ibid., 44.

26. Of course, what this assumes is a *heterosexual* gaze. Later theorists have challenged this heterosexist position and have rethought theories of the gaze within a broader framework. We will take up some of these criticisms and new interventions later.

27. Laura Mulvey, "Afterthoughts on 'Visual Pleasure and Narrative Cinema' . . . Inspired by *Duel in Sun*," *Framework* 15/16/17 (1981): 3–10, reprinted in Mulvey, *Visual and Other Pleasures*, 29–38.

28. Carroll, "The Image of Women in Film," 351.

29. Devereaux, "Oppressive Texts, Resisting Readers, and the Gendered Spectator," 341.

30. Judith Mayne, *The Woman at the Keyhole: Feminism and Women's Cinema* (Bloomington: Indiana University Press, 1990), 16.

31. Mulvey, *Visual and Other Pleasures*, 17.

32. Kaplan, "Feminist Criticism and Television," 230.

33. John Ellis, *Visible Fictions* (London: Routledge and Kegan Paul, 1982), 160.

34. Dan Rubey, "Voguing at the Carnival: Desire and Pleasure on MTV," *South Atlantic Quarterly* 90, no. 4 (fall 1991): 892.

35. One could point to recent work, such as Naomi Wolf's on "the beauty myth," that uses the concept of the male gaze without necessarily invoking its complex psychoanalytic heritage (Naomi Wolf, *The Beauty Myth* [New York: William Morrow, 1991]).

36. Coward, *Female Desires*.

37. Susanne Kappeler, *The Pornography of Representation* (Cambridge: Polity Press, 1986), 61.

3. Positioning Women

1. Kuhn, *Women's Pictures*, 28.

2. The importance of Althusser for cultural studies should not be underestimated. Althusser's work on ideology created a new and invigorated concern with those areas (culture, education, family, subjectivity) typically considered by left critics as "subordinate" to the more crucial areas of the economy and the workings of capital. Ideology becomes, in Althusser's rereading of Marx, not something simply "false" and imposed on the "masses" by the ruling class, but instead something quite real that we all "live through." In allowing ideology to be somewhat "set off" from the economic base, Althusser gave much more credence to the analysis of the production of meaning through cultural activity. Much has been written about the impact of Althusser on left cultural criticism; see especially Richard Johnson, "What Is Cultural Studies, Anyway?" *Social Text* 16 (winter 1986–87): 38–80.

3. Christine Gledhill, "The Melodramatic Field: An Investigation," in *Home Is Where the Heart Is: Studies in Melodrama and the Woman's Film*, ed. Christine Gledhill (London: British Film Institute, 1987), 8.

4. Kuhn, *Women's Pictures*, 36.

5. Ellis, *Visible Fictions*, 74–75.

6. Shaun Moores, "Texts, Readers and Contexts of Meaning:

Developments in the Study of Media Audiences," *Media, Culture and Society* 12 (1990): 12.

7. Kuhn, *Women's Pictures*, 32.

8. Gillian Dyer, "Women and Television: An Overview," in *Boxed In: Women and Television*, ed. Helen Baehr and Gillian Dyer (London: Pandora Press, 1987), 11.

9. De Lauretis, *Alice Doesn't*, 140.

10. Kuhn, *Women's Pictures*, 34.

11. Ibid., 35.

12. Judith Mayne, "The Female Audience and the Feminist Critic," in *Women and Film*, ed. Janet Todd (New York: Holmes and Meier, 1988), 24.

13. Much has been made of Dietrich's costuming in the film; indeed, her masculine attire is always present at her most self-defining (and therefore "unfeminine") moments.

14. Ellis, *Visible Fictions*, 158.

15. Martha Nochimson, *No End to Her: Soap Opera and the Female Subject* (Berkeley and Los Angeles: University of California Press, 1992), 30.

16. Moores, "Texts, Readers and Contexts of Meaning," 20–21.

17. Mayne, "The Female Audience and the Feminist Critic," 27–28.

18. Stuart Hall, "Encoding/Decoding," in *Culture, Media, Language: Working Papers in Cultural Studies, 1972–79*, ed. Stuart Hall et al. (London: Hutchinson, 1980).

19. Ien Ang, *Watching Dallas: Soap Opera and the Melodramatic Imagination* (London: Methuen, 1985), 119.

20. Ibid.

21. Nochimson, *No End to Her*, 2.

22. Annette Kuhn, "Women's Genres," *Screen* 25, no. 1 (1984): 20.

23. Tania Modleski, *Loving with a Vengeance: Mass-Produced Fantasies for Women* (New York: Methuen, 1982), 111.

24. Kuhn, "Women's Genres," 18.

25. Mary Ann Doane, "The 'Woman's Film': Possession and

Address," in Doane, Mellencamp, and Williams, *Re-Vision: Essays in Feminist Film Criticism*, 70.

26. Maria LaPlace, "Producing and Consuming the Woman's Film," in Gledhill, *Home Is Where the Heart Is*, 139.

27. Linda Williams, "Something Else besides a Mother: *Stella Dallas* and the Maternal Melodrama," in Gledhill, *Home Is Where the Heart Is*, 305.

28. Gledhill, "The Melodramatic Field: An Investigation," 37.

29. Jackie Byars, "Gazes/Voices/Power: Expanding Psychoanalysis for Feminist Film and Television Theory," in Pribram, *Female Spectators*, 121.

30. Doane, *Femmes Fatales*, 103.

31. Ang, *Watching Dallas*, 134–35.

4. You Looking at Me?

1. Ann Gray, "Reading the Audience," *Screen* 28, no. 3 (1987): 24–25.

2. Betterton, "How Do Women Look?" 220.

3. Suzanne Moore, "Here's Looking at You, Kid!" in Gamman and Marshment, *The Female Gaze*, 49.

4. Doane, "The 'Woman's Film,'" 68.

5. E. Deidre Pribram, Introduction, in Pribram, *Female Spectators*, 1.

6. Laura Mulvey, "Afterthoughts on 'Visual Pleasure and Narrative Cinema' . . . Inspired by *Duel in the Sun*," *Framework* 15/16/17 (1981): 3–10, reprinted in Mulvey, *Visual and Other Pleasures*, 29–38.

7. Moore, "Here's Looking at You, Kid!" 49.

8. Janet Bergstrom and Mary Ann Doane, "The Female Spectator: Contexts and Directions," *Camera Obscura*, nos. 20–21 (May-September 1989): 8.

9. Kuhn, "Women's Genres," 23.

10. Rosalind Brunt, "Engaging with the Popular: Audiences for Mass Culture and What to Say about Them," in *Cultural Studies*, ed. Lawrence Grossberg, Cary Nelson, and Paula Treichler (New York: Routledge, 1992), 69.

11. Gray, "Reading the Audience," 33.

12. This interesting and productive tack attempts to widen our understanding of "audience" and "interpretation" beyond both the individual, idiosyncratic consumer and the all-determining text. This multilayered method seems most promising, as will be discussed in later chapters.

13. Rhona Berenstein, "Individual Responses," *Camera Obscura*, nos. 20–21 (May-September 1989): 92.

14. Charlotte Brunsdon, "Individual Responses," *Camera Obscura*, nos. 20–21 (May-September 1989): 109.

15. Jeanne Allen, "Looking through 'Rear Window': Hitchcock's Traps and Lures of Heterosexual Romance," in Pribram, *Female Spectators*, 33.

16. Lorraine Gamman, "Watching the Detectives: The Enigma of the Female Gaze," in Gamman and Marshment, *The Female Gaze*, 12.

17. Ibid., 19.

18. Ibid., 15.

19. Elizabeth Long, "Women, Reading, and Cultural Authority: Some Implications of the Audience Perspective in Cultural Studies," *American Quarterly* 38, no. 4 (fall 1986): 593.

20. Jane Feuer, "Melodrama, Serial Form, and Television Today," *Screen* 25, no. 1 (1984): 15.

21. Lucie Arbuthnot and Gail Seneca, "Pre-Text and Text in "*Gentlemen Prefer Blondes*," in Erens, *Issues in Feminist Film Criticism*, 112.

22. Ibid., 113.

23. Ibid.

24. Lisa Lewis, "Consumer Girl Culture: How Music Video Appeals to Girls," in *Television and Women's Culture: The Politics of the Popular*, ed. Mary Ellen Brown (Newbury Park, Calif.: Sage, 1990), 89, 97.

25. Ibid., 91.

26. Andrea Weiss, "'A Queer Feeling When I Look at You'— Hollywood Stars and Lesbian Spectatorship in the 1930s," in

Stardom: Industry of Desire, ed. Christine Gledhill (London: Routledge, 1991), 293.

27. Ibid., 290.

28. Bergstrom and Doane, "The Female Spectator," 11.

29. Ibid., 12.

30. Janice Radway, "Identifying Ideological Seams: Mass Culture, Analytic Method, and Political Practice," *Communication* 9, no. 1 (1986): 99.

31. Janice Radway, *Reading the Romance: Women, Patriarchy, and Popular Literature* (Chapel Hill: University of North Carolina Press, 1984), 8.

32. Janice Radway, Introduction [new], *Reading the Romance* (Chapel Hill: University of North Carolina Press, 1991), 7.

33. Brown, *Television and Women's Culture*.

34. Dorothy Hobson, "Women Audiences and the Workplace," in Brown, *Television and Women's Culture*, 62.

35. Ibid.

36. Ibid., 65.

37. Jacqueline Bobo, "*The Color Purple*: Black Women as Cultural Readers," in Pribram, *Female Spectators*, 93.

38. Ibid., 101.

39. Ibid., 107.

40. Moores, "Texts, Readers and Contexts of Reading," 14.

41. Constance Penley, "Feminism, Psychoanalysis, and the Study of Popular Culture," in Grossberg, Nelson, and Treichler, *Cultural Studies*, 479–500.

42. Brunt, "Engaging with the Popular," 76.

43. Janet Lee, "Subversive Sitcoms: *Roseanne* as Inspiration for Feminist Resistance," *Women's Studies* 21 (1992): 87.

44. Laurie Schulze, "On the Muscle," in Gaines and Herzog, *Fabrications: Costume and the Female Body*, 66.

45. Ibid.

46. Ibid.

47. Annette Kuhn, "The Body and Cinema: Some Problems for Feminism," in *Grafts: Feminist Cultural Criticism*, ed. Susan Sheridan (London: Verso, 1988), 16.

48. Ibid., 19.

49. Elizabeth Ellsworth, "Illicit Pleasures: Feminist Spectators and *Personal Best*," in Erens, *Issues in Feminist Film Criticism*, 183.

50. Lynn Spigel and Denise Mann, eds., *Private Screenings: Television and the Female Consumer* (Minneapolis: University of Minnesota Press, 1992), vii.

51. Kuhn, "Women's Genres," 23.

52. Ibid., 24.

53. Gray, "Reading the Audience," 28.

54. Meaghan Morris, "Banality in Cultural Studies," in *Logics of Television: Essays in Cultural Criticism*, ed. Patricia Mellencamp (Bloomington: Indiana University Press, 1990), 21, 23.

55. Ibid., 24–25.

56. Jacqueline Bobo and Ellen Seiter, "Black Feminism and Media Criticism: *The Women of Brewster Place*," *Screen* 32, no. 3 (autumn 1991): 290.

57. Christine Gledhill, "Pleasurable Negotiations," in Pribram, *Female Spectators*, 67–68.

58. Ibid., 71.

59. Andrea Press, *Women Watching Television: Gender, Class, and Generation in the American Television Experience* (Philadelphia: University of Pennsylvania Press, 1991), 177.

60. Byars, *All That Hollywood Allows*, 31.

61. Ibid.

5. Postfeminism and Popular Culture

1. These two terms, *postmodernism* and *poststructuralism*, are difficult to define and no summary phrase emerges easily. We could say for our purposes here, however, that these frameworks have taken issue with many of the "truths" originated in Enlightenment philosophy, particularly those concerned with the nature of reason and the narratives of inevitable progress. Poststructuralism emphasizes the centrality of language in not simply reflecting meaning, but actually determining it. In addi-

tion, poststructuralism challenges the idea of unitary subjectivity, and argues instead for a notion of the subject as constructed by discourse and therefore necessarily fragmented and partial. In that sense, the theory of identity politics must be suspect, as it presupposes a self that has an identity, whereas poststructuralists would argue that the notion of identity itself is a fiction.

2. Susan Bolotin, "Voices from the Post-Feminist Generation," *New York Times Magazine*, 17 October 1982, 31.

3. Claudia Wallis, "Onward, Women!" *Time*, 4 December 1989, 81.

4. Ibid., 80–81.

5. It is thus no accident that much of the postfeminist backlash centers around rethinking motherhood. This rethinking, ironically enough, is more like a regression, whereby women are constantly barraged with images of their incipient "childlessness" and encouraged to blame feminism for not warning them of the perils of keeping time to a clock that is other than biological.

6. Betty Friedan, *The Feminine Mystique* (New York: Dell Publishing, 1963).

7. Betty Friedan, *The Second Stage* (New York: Summit Books, 1981).

8. Geneva Overholser, "What 'Post-Feminism' Really Means," *New York Times*, 19 September 1986, A34.

9. Daphne Merkin, "Prince Charming Comes Back," *New York Times Magazine*, 15 July 1990, 18, 20.

10. Ibid., 20.

11. Robert Lapsley and Michael Westlake, "From *Casablanca* to *Pretty Woman*: The Politics of Romance," *Screen* 33, no. 1 (spring 1992): 28.

12. Harvey Roy Greenberg, "Re-screwed: Pretty Woman's Co-opted Feminism," *Journal of Popular Film and Television* 19 (spring 1991): 10.

13. Ibid., 11.

14. Jane Caputi, "Sleeping with the Enemy as Pretty Woman, Part II?" *Journal of Popular Film and Television* 19 (spring 1991): 4, 5.

15. Georgia Brown, "On Their Case," *Village Voice*, 7 August 1990, 68.

16. Joy Horowitz, "Poof! The Mommies Vanish in Sitcomland," *New York Times*, 26 May 1991, 23.

17. Judith Stacey, "Sexism by a Subtler Name? Postindustrial Conditions and Postfeminist Consciousness in Silicon Valley," in *Women, Class, and the Feminist Imagination: A Socialist-Feminist Reader*, ed. Karen V. Hansen and Ilene J. Philipson (Philadelphia: Temple University Press, 1990), 339.

18. Rayna Rapp, "Is the Legacy of Second-Wave Feminism Postfeminism?" in Hansen and Philipson, *Women, Class, and the Feminist Imagination*, 358.

6. Material Girls

1. Pribram, Introduction, in Pribram, *Female Spectators*, 2–3.

2. Further work in this area would include an attempt to make more explicit connections between feminist social theory and feminist theories of representation. Up until now, the two have been curiously separate. Nancy Hartsock's idea of a "feminist standpoint" could perhaps be taken up by feminist cultural critics to explore the specificity of women's relationship to cultural imagery; see Hartsock, *Money, Sex and Power: Towards Feminist Historical Materialism* (Boston: Northeastern University Press, 1983).

3. Michele Barrett, "Representation and Cultural Production," in *Ideology and Cultural Production*, ed. Michele Barrett et al. (New York: St. Martin's Press, 1979), 12.

4. Tania Modleski, "Femininity as Mas(s)querade: A Feminist Approach to Mass Culture," in MacCabe, *High Theory / Low Culture*, 51.

5. Leslie Stern, "Feminism and Cinema: Exchanges," *Screen* 20, nos. 3–4 (1979–80): 89–90.

6. Elizabeth G. Traube, *Dreaming Identities: Class, Gender, and Generation in 1980s Hollywood Movies* (Boulder: Westview Press, 1992), 11.

7. Bergstrom and Doane, "The Female Spectator," 8.

8. Modleski, *Loving with a Vengeance*, 29.

9. Michele Barrett, "Ideology and the Cultural Production of Gender," in *Feminist Criticism and Social Change: Sex, Class and Race in Literature and Culture*, ed. Judith Newton and Deborah Rosenfelt (New York: Methuen, 1985), 75.

10. Rosemary Betterton, "Introduction: Feminism, Femininity and Representation," in Betterton, *Looking On: Images of Femininity in the Visual Arts and Media*, 1–2.

11. The history of the CCCS in its negotiation with traditional academic life as well as with the theoretical grab bag proffered by the new social movements of the 1960s and 1970s is long and contested. Although there is not a single "Birmingham School," the development has been characterized by certain central debates and issues, not least among them the question of structuralism and the relative autonomy of culture, à la Althusser. For solid introductions to these debates, see Johnson, "What Is Cultural Studies, Anyway?"; Stuart Hall, "Cultural Studies: Two Paradigms," *Media, Culture and Society* 2 (1980): 57–72; and CCCS texts such as Stuart Hall, Dorothy Hobson, Andrew Lowe, and Paul Willis, eds., *Culture, Media, Language: Working Papers in Cultural Studies, 1972–79* (London: Hutchinson, 1980), and Stuart Hall and Tony Jefferson, eds., *Resistance through Rituals* (London: Hutchinson, 1976).

12. Kuhn, *Women's Pictures*, 77,95.

13. Gray, "Reading the Audience," 28.

14. See Angela McRobbie and Jenny Garber, "Girls and Subculture," in Hall and Jefferson, *Resistance through Rituals*, 209–22.

15. Ang, *Watching Dallas*.

16. David Morley, *Family Television: Cultural Power and Domestic Leisure* (London: Comedia, 1986).

17. Janice Radway, "Reception Study: Ethnography and the Problems of Dispersed Audiences and Nomadic Subjects," *Cultural Studies* 2, no. 3 (1988): 368–70.

18. Ibid., 366.

Bibliography

Adams, Parveen. "A Note on the Distinction between Sexual Division and Sexual Differences." *m/f* 4 (1979): 51–57.

———. "Representation and Sexuality." *m/f* 1 (1978): 65–82.

Adorno, Theodor. "Culture Industry Reconsidered." *New German Critique* 6 (fall 1976): 12–19.

———. *Prisms*. London: Neville Spearman, 1967.

Agger, Ben. *Cultural Studies as Critical Theory*. London: Falmer Press, 1992.

Alcoff, Linda. "Cultural Feminism versus Post-Structuralism: The Identity Crisis in Feminist Theory." *Signs* 13, no. 3 (1988): 405–36.

Allen, Jeanne. "Looking through 'Rear Window': Hitchcock's Traps and Lures of Heterosexual Romance." In *Female Spectators: Looking at Film and Television*, edited by E. Deidre Pribram, 31–44. London: Verso, 1988.

Allen, Robert C., editor. *Channels of Discourse: Television and Contemporary Criticism*. Chapel Hill: University of North Carolina Press, 1987.

Ang, Ien. *Desperately Seeking the Audience*. London: Routledge, 1991.

———. *Watching Dallas: Soap Opera and the Melodramatic Imagination*. London: Methuen, 1985.

Angus, Ian, and Sut Jhally, editors. *Cultural Politics in Contemporary America*. New York: Routledge, 1989.

Arato, Andrew, and Eike Gebhardt, editors. *The Essential Frankfurt School Reader*. Oxford: Blackwell, 1978.

Arbuthnot, Lucie, and Gail Seneca. "Pre-Text and Text in *Gentlemen Prefer Blondes*." In *Issues in Feminist Film Criticism*, edited by Patricia Erens, 112–25. Bloomington: Indiana University Press, 1990.

Atkin, David J., Jay Moorman, and Carolyn A. Lin. "Ready for Prime Time: Network Series Devoted to Working Women." *Sex Roles* 25 (1991): 677–85.

Baehr, Helen. "The Impact of Feminism on Media Studies—Just Another Commercial Break?" In *Men's Studies Modified: The Impact of Feminism on the Academic Disciplines*, edited by Dale Spender, 141–54. New York: Athene Series/Pergamon Press, 1981.

Baehr, Helen, and Gillian Dyer, editors. *Boxed In: Women and Television*. London: Pandora Press, 1987.

Bagdikian, Ben. *The Information Machines: Their Impact on Men in the Media*. New York: Harper and Row, 1971.

Balsamo, Anne. "Feminism and Cultural Studies." *Journal of the Midwest Modern Language Association* 24, no. 1 (1991): 50–73.

Barnouw, Erik. *The Sponsor: Notes on a Modern Potentate*. Oxford: Oxford University Press, 1978.

———. *Tube of Plenty: The Evolution of American Television*. Oxford: Oxford University Press, 1975.

Barrett, Michele. "Ideology and the Cultural Production of Gender." In *Feminist Criticism and Social Change: Sex, Class and Race in Literature and Culture*, edited by Judith Newton and Deborah Rosenfelt, 65–85. New York: Methuen, 1985.

———. "Representation and Cultural Production." In *Ideology and Cultural Production*, edited by Michele Barrett, Philip Corrigan, Annette Kuhn, and Janet Woolf, 9–24. New York: St. Martin's Press, 1979.

———. *Women's Oppression Today*. London: New Left Books/Verso, 1980.

Barrett, Michele, Philip Corrigan, Annette Kuhn, and Janet

Woolf, editors. *Ideology and Cultural Production*. New York: St. Martin's Press, 1979.

Barthel, Diane. *Putting on Appearances: Gender and Advertising*. Philadelphia: Temple University Press, 1988.

Barthes, Roland. *Elements of Semiology*. London: Jonathan Cape, 1967.

———. *The Fashion System*. Berkeley and Los Angeles: University of California Press, 1983.

Bathrick, Serafina. "The Mary Tyler Moore Show: Women at Home and at Work." In *MTM: Quality Television*, edited by Jane Feuer, Paul Kerr, and Tise Vahimagi, 99–131. London: British Film Institute, 1984.

Baudrillard, Jean. *The Ecstasy of Communication*. New York: Semiotext(e), 1987.

———. *For a Critique of the Political Economy of the Sign*. St. Louis: Telos, 1981.

———. *In the Shadow of the Silent Majorities*. New York: Semiotext(e), 1983.

———. *Simulations*. New York: Semiotext(e), 1983.

Benjamin, Walter. *Illuminations*. London: Fontana, 1973.

Bennett, Tony. *Outside Literature*. New York: Routledge, 1990.

Bennett, Tony, Susan Boyd-Bowman, Colin Mercer, and Janet Woollacott, editors. *Popular Television and Film*. London: British Film Institute with the Open University Press, 1981.

Berenstein, Rhona. "Individual Responses." *Camera Obscura*, nos. 20–21 (May-September 1989): 88–93.

Berger, John. *The Sense of Sight*. New York: Pantheon, 1985.

———. *Ways of Seeing*. London: British Broadcasting Corporation, and Harmondsworth: Penguin, 1972.

Bergstrom, Janet, and Mary Ann Doane. "The Female Spectator: Contexts and Directions." *Camera Obscura*, nos. 20–21 (May-September 1989): 5–27.

Besharov, Douglas. "Beyond Murphy Brown." *Washington Post*, 27 June 1992, C3.

Best, Steven. "The Commodification of Reality and the Reality of Commodification: Jean Baudrillard and Post-Modernism." *Current Perspectives in Social Theory* 9 (1989): 23–51.

Betterton, Rosemary. "How Do Women Look? The Female Nude in the Work of Suzanne Valadon." In *Looking On: Images of Femininity in the Visual Arts and Media*, edited by Rosemary Betterton, 217–34. London. Pandora Press, 1987.

———. "Introduction: Feminism, Femininity and Representation." In *Looking On: Images of Femininity in the Visual Arts and Media*, edited by Rosemary Betterton, 1–17. London: Pandora Press, 1987.

———. "A Question of Difference." *Screen* 26, nos. 3–4 (May–August 1985): 102–9.

———, editor. *Looking On: Images of Femininity in the Visual Arts and Media*. London: Pandora Press, 1987.

Bobo, Jacqueline. "*The Color Purple*: Black Women as Cultural Readers." In *Female Spectators: Looking at Film and Television*, edited by E. Deidre Pribram, 90–109. London: Verso, 1988.

———. "Individual Responses." *Camera Obscura*, nos. 20–21 (May–September 1989): 100–103.

Bobo, Jacqueline, and Ellen Seiter. "Black Feminism and Media Criticism: *The Women of Brewster Place*." *Screen* 32, no. 3 (autumn 1991): 286–302.

Bodroghkozy, Aniko. "'Is This What You Mean by Color TV?': Race, Gender, and Contested Meanings in NBC's *Julia*." In *Private Screenings: Television and the Female Consumer*, edited by Lynn Spigel and Denise Mann, 143–67. Minneapolis: University of Minnesota Press, 1992.

Bogle, Donald. *Toms, Coons, Mulattoes, Mammies and Bucks: An Interpretive History of Blacks in American Films*. New York: Continuum, 1989.

Bolotin, Susan. "Voices from the Post-Feminist Generation." *New York Times Magazine*, 17 October 1982, 31.

Boorstin, Daniel J. *The Image: A Guide to Pseudo-Events in America*. New York: Harper Colophon, 1961.

Bordwell, David, and Kristin Thompson. *Film Art*. Reading, Mass.: Addison-Wesley, 1979.

Brantlinger, Patrick. *Crusoe's Footprints. Cultural Studies in Britain and America*. New York: Routledge, 1990.

Braudy, Leo. *The World in a Frame: What We See in Film*. Chicago: University of Chicago Press, 1976.

Brown, Georgia. "On Their Case." *Village Voice*, 7 August 1990, 68.

Brown, Jane, and Laurie Schulz. "The Effects of Race, Gender, and Fandom on Audience Interpretations of Madonna's Music Videos." *Journal of Communication* 40 (spring 1990): 88–102.

Brown, Mary Ellen. "Consumption and Resistance—The Problem of Pleasure." In *Television and Women's Culture: The Politics of the Popular*, edited by Mary Ellen Brown, 201–10. Newbury Park, Calif.: Sage, 1990.

———, editor. *Television and Women's Culture: The Politics of the Popular*. Newbury Park, Calif.: Sage, 1990.

Brunsdon, Charlotte. "Individual Responses." *Camera Obscura*, nos. 20–21 (May-September 1989): 108–10.

———, editor. *Films for Women*. London: British Film Institute, 1986.

Brunt, Rosalind. "Engaging with the Popular: Audiences for Mass Culture and What to Say about Them." In *Cultural Studies*, edited by Lawrence Grossberg, Cary Nelson, and Paula Treichler, 69–80. New York: Routledge, 1992.

Brunt, Rosalind, and Caroline Rowan. *Feminism, Culture and Politics*. London: Lawrence and Wishart, 1982.

Buhle, Paul, editor. *Popular Culture in America*. Minneapolis: University of Minnesota Press, 1987.

Burger, Peter. *Theory of the Avant-Garde*. Manchester: Manchester University Press, 1984.

Busby, Linda J. "Sex-Role Research on the Mass Media." *Journal of Communication* 25, no. 4 (autumn 1975): 107–31.

Butsch, Richard, editor. *For Fun and Profit: The Transformation of Leisure into Consumption*. Philadelphia: Temple University Press, 1990.

Byars, Jackie. *All That Hollywood Allows: Re-reading Gender in 1950s Melodrama*. Chapel Hill: University of North Carolina Press, 1991.

———. "Gazes/Voices/Power: Expanding Psychoanalysis for Feminist Film and Television Theory." In *Female Spectators: Looking at Film and Television*, edited by E. Deidre Pribram, 110–31. London: Verso, 1988.

———. "Gender/Marginalized Discourse/Mainstream Narrative." Paper presented at the Sixth International Conference on Culture and Communication, Philadelphia, October 1986.

———. "Reading Feminine Discourse: Prime-Time Television in the U.S." *Communication* 9 (1987): 289–303.

Cantwell, Mary. "What Were the Women 'Asking' For?" *New York Times*, 13 June 1991, A28.

Caputi, Jane. "Sleeping with the Enemy as Pretty Woman, Part II?" *Journal of Popular Film and Television* 19 (spring 1991): 2–8.

Carlson, Margaret. "Is This What Feminism Is All About?" *Time*, 24 June 1991, 57.

Carr, Helen. *From My Guy to Sci-Fi: Genre and Women's Writing in the Postmodern World*. London: Pandora Press, 1989.

Carroll, Noel. "The Image of Women in Film: A Defence of a Paradigm." *Journal of Aesthetics and Art Criticism* 48 (fall 1990): 349–60.

Castleman, Harry, and Walter J. Podrazik. *Watching TV: Four Decades of American Television*. New York: McGraw-Hill, 1982.

Caughie, John. "Television Criticism: 'A Discourse in Search of an Object.'" *Screen* 25, nos. 4–5 (July–October 1984): 109–20.

Cawelti, John. *Adventure, Mystery, and Romance*. Chicago: University of Chicago Press, 1976.

Centre for Contemporary Cultural Studies, Women's Studies Group. *Women Take Issue*. London: Hutchinson, 1978.

Christian-Smith, Linda. *Becoming a Woman through Romance.* New York: Routledge, 1990.

Clarke, John, Chas Critcher, and Richard Johnson, editors. *Working-Class Culture: Studies in History and Theory.* London: Hutchinson, 1979.

Clover, C. J. "Her Body, Himself: Gender in the Slasher Film." *Representations* 20 (fall 1987): 187–228.

Cohen, Stanley. *Folk Devils and Moral Panics: The Creation of the Mods and Rockers.* London: MacGibbon and Kee, 1972.

Cohen, Stanley, and Jock Young. *The Manufacture of News: Deviance, Social Problems and the Mass Media.* London: Constable, 1973.

Collins, Jim. *Uncommon Cultures: Popular Culture and Post-Modernism.* New York: Routledge, 1989.

Collins, Jim, Hilary Radner, and Ava Preacher Collins, editors. *Film Theory Goes to the Movies.* New York: Routledge, 1993.

Connor, Steven. *Postmodernist Culture: An Introduction to Theories of the Contemporary.* Cambridge, Mass.: Basil Blackwell, 1989.

Considine, David. *The Cinema of Adolescence.* Jefferson, N.C.: McFarland, 1985.

Cook, Pam, editor. *The Cinema Book.* New York: Pantheon, 1986.

Courtney, Alice, and Thomas Whipple. "Women in TV Commercials." *Journal of Communication* (spring 1974): 110–18.

Coward, Rosalind. *Female Desires: How They Are Sought, Bought and Packaged.* New York: Grove Press, 1985.

Coward, Rosalind, and John Ellis. *Language and Materialism: Developments in Semiology and the Theory of the Subject.* Boston: Routledge and Kegan Paul, 1977.

Cowie, Elizabeth. "Woman as Sign." *m/f* 1 (1978): 49–63.

———. "Women, Representation and the Image." *Screen Education* 23 (summer 1977): 15–23.

Creed, Barbara. "From Here to Modernity: Feminism and Postmodernism." *Screen* 28, no. 2 (spring 1987): 47–67.

———. "Pornography and Pleasure: The Female Spectator." *Australian Journal of Screen Theory* 15–16 (1983): 27–31.

Creedon, Pamela, editor. *Women in Mass Communication: Challenging Gender Values*. London: Sage, 1989.

Culler, Jonathan. *Framing the Sign: Criticism and Its Institutions*. Norman: University of Oklahoma Press, 1988.

Cummings, Melbourne. "The Changing Image of the Black Family on Television." *Journal of Popular Culture* 22, no. 2 (fall 1988): 75–85.

Curran, James, Michael Gurevitch, and Janet Woollacott, editors. *Mass Communication and Society*. London: Sage, 1979.

Dargis, Manohla. "Guns N' Poses," *Village Voice*, 16 July 1991, 22.

Davies, Kath, Julienne Dickey, and Teresa Stratford, editors. *Out of Focus: Writings on Women and the Media*. London: The Women's Press, 1987.

Debord, Guy. *Society of the Spectacle*. 1967; Detroit: Black and Red, 1977.

de Lauretis, Teresa. "Aesthetic and Feminist Theory: Rethinking Women's Cinema." In *Female Spectators: Looking at Film and Television*, edited by E. Deidre Pribram, 174–75. London: Verso, 1988.

———. *Alice Doesn't: Feminism, Semiotics, Cinema*. Bloomington: Indiana University Press, 1984.

———. "Guerilla in the Midst: Women's Cinema in the 80s." *Screen* 31, no. 2 (spring 1990): 6–25.

———. *"Technologies of Gender: Essays on Theory, Film, and Fiction*. Bloomington: Indiana University Press, 1987.

———, editor. *Feminist Studies/Critical Studies*. Bloomington: Indiana University Press, 1986.

Descombes, Vincent. *Modern French Philosophy*. Cambridge: Cambridge University Press, 1979.

Devereaux, Mary. "Oppressive Texts, Resisting Readers, and the Gendered Spectator: The New Aesthetics." *Journal of Aesthetics and Art Criticism* 48, no. 4 (fall 1990): 337–48.

Dittmar, Linda. "Beyond Gender and within It: The Social Construction of Female Desire." *Wide Angle* 8, no. 4 (1986): 79–90.

Doane, Mary Ann. *The Desire to Desire: The Women's Film of the 1940s*. Bloomington: Indiana University Press, 1987.

———. "The Economy of Desire: The Commodity Form in/of the Cinema." *Quarterly Review of Film and Video* 11 (1989): 23–33.

———. *Femmes Fatales: Feminism, Film Theory, Psychoanalysis*. New York: Routledge, 1991.

———. "Film and Masquerade: Theorizing the Female Spectator." *Screen* 23 (September-October): 74–87. Reprinted in *Issues in Feminist Film Criticism*, edited by Patricia Erens, 41–57, Bloomington: Indiana University Press, 1990.

———. "The 'Woman's Film': Possession and Address." In *Re-Vision: Essays in Feminist Film Criticism*, edited by Mary Ann Doane, Patricia Mellencamp, and Linda Williams, 67–82. Los Angeles: American Film Institute, 1984.

———. "Woman's Stake: Filming the Female Body." *October* 17 (summer 1981): 22–36. Reprinted in *Feminism and Film Theory*, edited by Constance Penley, 216–28, New York: Routledge, 1988.

Doane, Mary Ann, Patricia Mellencamp, and Linda Williams. "Feminist Film Criticism: An Introduction." In *Re-Vision: Essays in Feminist Film Criticism*, edited by Mary Ann Doane, Patricia Mellencamp, and Linda Williams, 1–15. Los Angeles: American Film Institute, 1984.

Doane, Mary Ann, Patricia Mellencamp, and Linda Williams, editors. *Re-Vision: Essays in Feminist Film Criticism*. Los Angeles: American Film Institute, 1984.

Dominick, J. R. "The Portrayal of Women in Prime-Time, 1953–1977." *Sex Roles* 5 (1979): 405–11.

Donaldson, Laura. "(ex)Changing (wo)Man: Towards a Materialist-Feminist Semiotics." *Cultural Critique* 11 (winter 1988–89): 5–23.

Downing, Mildred. "Heroine of the Daytime Serial." *Journal of Communication* 24, no. 2 (spring 1974): 130–37.

Dyer, Gillian. "Women and Television: An Overview." In *Boxed*

In: Women and Television, edited by Helen Baehr and Gillian Dyer, 6–16. London: Pandora Press, 1987.

Dyer, Richard. *Stars*. London: British Film Institute, 1979.

Eagleton, Terry. *Criticism and Ideology*. London: Verso, 1976.

———. *Ideology: An Introduction*. London: Verso, 1991.

———. *Literary Theory*. Minneapolis: University of Minnesota Press, 1983.

Ecker, Gisela, editor. *Feminist Aesthetics*. Boston: Beacon Press, 1985.

Eco, Umberto. *A Theory of Semiotics*. Bloomington: Indiana University Press, 1979.

Ehrenreich, Barbara. "The Undainty Feminism of Roseanne Barr: The Wretched of the Hearth." *New Republic*, 2 April 1990, 28–31.

Eisenstein, Hester, and Alice Jardine, editors. *The Future of Difference*. Boston: G. K. Hall, 1980.

Ellis, John. *Visible Fictions*. London: Routledge and Kegan Paul, 1982.

Ellsworth, Elizabeth. "Illicit Pleasures: Feminist Spectators and *Personal Best*." In *Issues in Feminist Film Criticism*, edited by Patricia Erens, 183–96. Bloomington: Indiana University Press, 1990.

Elsaesser, Thomas. "Tales of Sound and Fury: Observations on the Family Melodrama." In *Home Is Where the Heart Is: Studies in Melodrama and Women's Film*, edited by Christine Gledhill, 43–69. London: British Film Institute, 1987.

Erens, Patricia, editor. *Issues in Feminist Film Criticism*. Bloomington: Indiana University Press, 1990.

———. *Sexual Stratagems: The World of Women in Film*. New York: Horizon Press, 1979.

Faludi, Susan. *Backlash: The Undeclared War against American Women*. New York: Crown, 1991.

Featherstone, Mike. *Consumer Culture and Postmodernism*. London: Sage, 1991.

Fekete, John, editor. *Life after Postmodernism: Essays on Value and Culture*. New York: St. Martin's Press, 1987.

Felski, Rita. *Beyond Feminist Aesthetics: Feminist Literature and Social Change*. Cambridge, Mass.: Harvard University Press, 1989.

Ferguson, Marjorie. *Forever Feminine: Women's Magazines and the Cult of Femininity*. London: Heinemann, 1983.

Feuer, Jane. "Melodrama, Serial Form, and Television Today." *Screen* 25, no. 1 (1984): 4–16.

———. "Narrative Form in American Network Television." In *High Theory/Low Culture: Analyzing Popular Television and Film*, edited by Colin MacCabe, 101–14. New York: St. Martin's Press, 1986.

Fiore, Quentin, and Marshall McLuhan. *The Medium Is the Massage: An Inventory of Effects*. New York: Bantam, 1967.

Fischer, Lucy. *Shot/Countershot: Film Tradition and Women's Cinema*. Princeton: Princeton University Press, 1989.

Fishman, Mark. *Manufacturing the News*. Austin: University of Texas Press, 1980.

Fiske, John. *Introduction to Communication Studies*. London: Methuen, 1982.

———. *Reading the Popular*. Boston: Unwin Hyman, 1989.

———. *Television Culture*. London: Methuen, 1987.

———. *Understanding Popular Culture*. Boston: Unwin Hyman, 1989.

Fiske, John, and John Hartley. *Reading Television*. London: Methuen, 1978.

Fleck, Patrice. "The Silencing of Women in the Hollywood 'Feminist' Film: *The Accused*." *Post Script* 3, no. 3 (1990): 49–55.

Flynn, Elizabeth A., and Patrocinio P. Schweichart, editors. *Gender and Reading: Essays on Readers, Texts, and Contexts*. Baltimore: Johns Hopkins University Press, 1986.

Foster, Hal. *Recodings: Art, Spectacle, Cultural Politics*. Port Townsend, Wash.: Bay Press, 1985.

———, editor. *The Anti-Aesthetic: Essays on Postmodern Culture*. Port Townsend, Wash.: Bay Press, 1983.

Frank, Lisa, and Paul Smith, editors. *Madonnarama: Essays on Sex and Popular Culture*. Pittsburgh: Cleis Press, 1993.

Friedan, Betty. *The Feminine Mystique*. New York: Dell Publishing, 1963.

———. *The Second Stage*. New York: Summit Books, 1981.

Frith, Simon, editor. *Facing the Music: A Pantheon Guide to Popular Culture*. New York: Pantheon, 1988.

———. *The Sociology of Rock*. London: Constable, 1976.

———. *Sound Effects*. New York: Pantheon, 1983.

Gaines, Jane. "In the Service of Ideology: How Betty Grable's Legs Won the War." *Film Reader* 5 (1982): 47–59.

———. "White Privilege and Looking Relations: Race and Gender in Feminist Film Theory." *Cultural Critique* 4 (fall 1986): 59–79.

———. "Women and Representation: Can We Enjoy Alternative Pleasure?" In *American Media and Mass Culture*, edited by Donald Lazere, 357–72. Berkeley and Los Angeles: University of California Press, 1987.

Gaines, Jane, and Charlotte Herzog, editors. *Fabrications: Costume and the Female Body*. New York: Routledge, 1990.

Gamman, Lorraine. "Watching the Detectives: The Enigma of the Female Gaze." In *The Female Gaze: Women as Viewers of Popular Culture*, edited by Lorraine Gamman and Margaret Marshment, 1–26. London: The Women's Press, 1988.

Gamman, Lorraine, and Margaret Marshment, editors. *The Female Gaze: Women as Viewers of Popular Culture*. London: The Women's Press, 1988.

Garnham, Nicholas. *Capitalism and Communication: Global Culture and the Economics of Information*. London: Sage, 1990.

Gerbner, George. "The Dynamics of Cultural Resistance." In *Hearth and Home: Images of Women in the Mass Media*, edited by Gaye Tuchman, Arlene Kaplan Daniels, and James Benet, 46–50. New York: Oxford University Press, 1978.

Gilliam, Dorothy. "Quayle-Brown Nonsense Obscures Real Family Issues." *Washington Post*, 23 September 1992, B1.

Gitlin, Todd. *Inside Prime Time*. New York: Pantheon, 1983.

———. "Prime Time Ideology: The Hegemonic Process in Television Entertainment." *Social Problems* 26, no. 3 (February 1979): 251–66.

———. *Watching Television*. New York: Pantheon, 1986.

———. *The Whole World Is Watching: Mass Media in the Making and Unmaking of the New Left*. Berkeley and Los Angeles: University of California Press, 1980.

Gledhill, Christine. "The Melodramatic Field: An Investigation." In *Home Is Where the Heart Is: Studies in Melodrama and the Woman's Film*, edited by Christine Gledhill, 5–42. London: British Film Institute, 1987.

———. "Pleasurable Negotiations." In *Female Spectators: Looking at Film and Television*, edited by E. Deidre Pribram, 64–89. London: Verso, 1988.

———, editor. *Home Is Where the Heart Is: Studies in Melodrama and the Woman's Film*. London: British Film Institute, 1987.

———. *Stardom: Industry of Desire*. London: Routledge, 1991.

Glennon, Lynda, and Richard Butsch. "The Family as Portrayed on Television 1946–1978." In *Television and Behavior: Ten Years of Scientific Progress and Implications for the Eighties*, United States Department of Health and Human Services, vol. 2, *Technical Reviews*, 264–71. Washington, D.C.: U.S. Government Printing Office, 1982.

Goffman, Erving. *Gender Advertisements*. New York: Harper Colophon Books / Harper and Row, 1976.

Gray, Ann. "Reading the Audience." *Screen* 28, no. 3 (1987): 24–35.

Greenberg, Harvey Roy. "Re-screwed: Pretty Woman's Co-opted Feminism." *Journal of Popular Film and Television* 19 (spring 1991): 9–13.

Grossberg, Lawrence, Cary Nelson, and Paula Treichler, editors. *Cultural Studies*. New York: Routledge, 1992.

Gurevitch, Michael, Tony Bennett, James Curran, and Janet Woollacott, editors. *Culture, Society and the Media*. London: Methuen, 1982.

Hall, Stuart. "Cultural Studies and Its Theoretical Legacies." In

Cultural Studies, edited by Lawrence Grossberg, Cary Nelson, and Paula Treichler, 277–94. New York: Routledge, 1992.

———. "Cultural Studies: Two Paradigms." *Media, Culture, and Society* 2 (1980): 57–72.

———. "The Emergence of Cultural Studies and the Crisis of the Humanities." *October* 53 (summer 1990): 11–90.

———. "Encoding/Decoding." In *Culture, Media, Language*, edited by Stuart Hall, Dorothy Hobson, Andrew Lowe, and Paul Willis, 128–38. London: Hutchinson, 1980.

———. "Notes on Deconstructing the Popular." In *People's History and Socialist Theory*, edited by Raphael Samuel, 227–39. London: Routledge, 1981.

Hall, Stuart, Chas Critcher, Tony Jefferson, John Clarke, and Brian Roberts. *Policing the Crisis*. London: Macmillan, 1978.

Hall, Stuart, Dorothy Hobson, Andrew Lowe, and Paul Willis, editors. *Culture, Media, Language: Working Papers in Cultural Studies, 1972–79*. London: Hutchinson, 1980.

Hall, Stuart, and Tony Jefferson, editors. *Resistance through Rituals*. London: Hutchinson, 1976.

Hall, Stuart, and Paddy Whannel. *The Popular Arts*. Boston: Beacon Press, 1964.

Hammel, William. *The Popular Arts in America: A Reader*. New York: Harcourt Brace Jovanovich, 1972.

Hansen, Karen V., and Ilene J. Philipson, editors. *Women, Class, and the Feminist Imagination: A Socialist-Feminist Reader*. Philadelphia: Temple University Press, 1990.

Haralovich, Mary Beth. "Advertising Heterosexuality." *Screen* 23, no. 2 (July-August 1982): 50–60.

———. "The Social History of Film: Heterogeneity and Mediation." *Wide Angle* 8, no. 2 (1986): 4–14.

Hartley, John. "Critical Response: The Real World of Audiences." *Critical Studies in Mass Communication* (September 1988): 234–38.

Hartsock, Nancy C. M. *Money, Sex and Power: Towards Feminist Historical Materialism*. Boston: Northeastern University Press, 1983.

Haskell, Molly. *From Reverence to Rape: The Treatment of Women in the Movies*. 2d edition. Chicago: University of Chicago Press, 1987.

Haug, Wolfgang Fritz. *Critique of Commodity Aesthetics: Appearance, Sexuality and Advertising in Capitalist Society*. Minneapolis: University of Minnesota Press, 1986.

Hawkes, Terence. *Structuralism and Semiotics*. London: Methuen, 1977.

Heath, Stephen. *Questions of Cinema*. Bloomington: Indiana University Press, 1981.

Heath, Stephen, and Teresa de Lauretis, editors. *The Cinematic Apparatus*. London: Macmillan, 1980.

Hebdige, Dick. *Subculture: The Meaning of Style*. London: Methuen, 1979.

Heck, Marina. "The Ideological Dimension of Media Messages." In *Culture, Media, Language: Working Papers in Cultural Studies, 1972–79*, edited by Stuart Hall, Dorothy Hobson, Andrew Lowe, and Paul Willis, 122–27. London: Hutchinson, 1980.

Heide, Margaret. "Mothering Ambivalence: The Treatment of Women's Gender Role Conflicts over Work and Family on *thirtysomething*." *Women's Studies* 21 (1992): 103–17.

Hilmes, Michelle. "Where Everybody Knows Your Name: *Cheers* and the Mediation of Cultures." *Wide Angle* 12, no. 2 (April 1990): 64–73.

Hobson, Dorothy. "Women Audiences and the Workplace." In *Television and Women's Culture: The Politics of the Popular*, edited by Mary Ellen Brown, 61–74. Newbury Park, Calif.: Sage, 1990.

Horowitz, Joy. "Poof! The Mommies Vanish in Sitcomland." *New York Times*, 26 May 1991, 23.

Hutcheon, Linda. *The Politics of Postmodernism*. New York: Routledge, 1989.

Huyssen, Andreas. *After the Great Divide: Modernism, Mass Culture, Postmodernism*. Bloomington: Indiana University Press, 1986.

Isaacs, Susan. "Sisterhood Isn't so Powerful in the Movies." *New York Times*, 14 January 1990, H1, H37.

Jameson, Fredric. *The Political Unconscious*. Ithaca: Cornell University Press, 1981.

———. "Postmodernism, or the Cultural Logic of Late Capitalism." *New Left Review* 146 (1984): 53–92.

Janus, Noreene Z. "Research on Sex-Roles in the Mass Media: Towards a Critical Approach." *Insurgent Sociologist* 7, no. 3 (summer 1977): 19–31.

Japp, Phyllis M. "Gender and Work in the 1980s: Television's Working Women as Displaced Persons." *Women's Studies in Communication* 14 (spring 1991): 49–74.

Jauss, Hans Robert. *Toward an Aesthetic of Reception*. Brighton, England: Harvester Press, 1982.

Jhally, Sut. *The Codes of Advertising: Fetishism and the Political Economy of Meaning in the Consumer Society*. New York: Routledge, 1990.

Johnson, Lesley. *The Cultural Critics: From Matthew Arnold to Raymond Williams*. London: Routledge and Kegan Paul, 1979.

Johnson, Richard. "What Is Cultural Studies, Anyway?" *Social Text* 16 (winter 1986–87): 38–80.

Johnston, Claire. "The Subject of Feminist Film Theory / Practice." *Screen* 21–22 (summer 1980): 27–34.

———, editor. *Notes on Women's Cinema*. London: Society for Education in Film and Television, 1973.

Johnston, Sheila. "Film Narrative and the Structuralist Controversy." In *The Cinema Book*, edited by Pam Cook, 222–51. New York: Pantheon, 1986.

Jones, Amelia. "'She Was Bad News': Male Paranoia and the Contemporary New Woman." *Camera Obscura*, nos. 25–26 (January-May 1991): 297–320.

Jones, Gerard. *Honey, I'm Home! Sitcoms: Selling the American Dream*. New York: St. Martin's Press, 1992.

Kahn, Coppelia, and Gayle Green, editors. *Making a Difference: Feminist Literary Criticism*. New York: Methuen, 1985.

Kahn, Douglas, and Diane Neumaier, editors. *Cultures in Contention*. Seattle: The Real Comet Press, 1985.

Kaler, Anne K. "*Golden Girls*: Feminine Archetypal Patterns of the Complete Woman." *Journal of Popular Culture* 24, no. 3 (winter 1990): 49–60.

Kaminsky, Stuart. *American Film Genres*. Chicago: Nelson-Hall, 1985.

Kaminsky, Stuart, and Jeffrey Mahan. *American Television Genres*. Chicago: Nelson-Hall, 1988.

Kaplan, E. Ann. "Feminist Criticism and Television." In *Channels of Discourse: Television and Contemporary Criticism*, edited by Robert C. Allen, 211–53. Chapel Hill: University of North Carolina Press, 1987.

———. "Mothering, Feminism and Representation: The Maternal in Melodrama and the Woman's Film 1910–1940." In *Home Is Where the Heart Is: Studies in Melodrama and the Woman's Film*, edited by Christine Gledhill, 113–37. London: British Film Institute, 1987.

———. "Movies and the Women's Movement." *Socialist Review*, no. 66 (November-December 1982): 78–89.

———. *Women and Film: Both Sides of the Camera*. New York: Methuen, 1983.

———, editor. *Postmodernism and Its Discontents: Theories, Practices*. New York: Verso, 1989.

———. *Regarding Television*. Frederick, Md.: University Publications of America, 1983.

———. *Women in Film Noir*. London: British Film Institute, 1978.

Kappeler, Susanne. *The Pornography of Representation*. Cambridge: Polity Press, 1986.

Kay, Karyn, and Gerry Peary, editors. *Women in the Cinema: A Critical Anthology*. New York: Dutton, 1977.

Kellner, Douglas. *Television and the Crisis of Democracy*. Boulder: Westview Press, 1990.

Kennedy, Lisa. "Risque Business: Fox TV Stoops to Conquer." *Village Voice*, 10 April 1990, 37.

King, Josephine, and Mary Stott. *Is This Your Life? Images of Women in the Media*. London: Virago, 1977.

Kipnis, Laura. "'Refunctioning' Reconsidered: Towards a Left Popular Culture." In *High Theory/Low Culture: Analyzing Popular Television and Film*, edited by Colin MacCabe, 11–36. New York: St. Martin's Press, 1986.

Kolbert, Elizabeth. "'Murphy Brown' Feud: When Art Replaces Life." *New York Times*, 23 September 1992, 21.

Kuhn, Annette. "The Body and Cinema: Some Problems for Feminism." In *Grafts: Feminist Cultural Criticism*, edited by Susan Sheridan, 11–23. London: Verso, 1988.

———. *The Power of the Image*. London: Routledge and Kegan Paul, 1985.

———. "Women's Genres." *Screen* 25, no. 1 (1984): 18–28.

———. *Women's Pictures: Feminism and Cinema*. London: Routledge and Kegan Paul, 1982.

———, editor. *Cultural Theory and Contemporary Science Fiction Cinema*. New York: Verso, 1990.

Kuhn, Annette, and Susannah Radstone, editors. *Women in Film: An International Guide*. New York: Fawcett Columbine, 1990.

LaPlace, Maria. "Producing and Consuming the Woman's Film." In *Home Is Where the Heart Is: Studies in Melodrama and the Woman's Film*, edited by Christine Gledhill, 138–66. London: British Film Institute, 1987.

Lapsley, Robert, and Michael Westlake. "From *Casablanca* to *Pretty Woman*: The Politics of Romance." *Screen* 33, no. 1 (spring 1992): 27–49.

Lauret, Maria. "Feminism and Culture—The Movie: A Critical Overview of Writing on Women and Cinema." *Women: A Cultural Review* 2, no. 1 (1991): 52–69.

Lazere, Donald, editor. *American Media and Mass Culture: Left Perspectives*. Berkeley and Los Angeles: University of California Press, 1987.

Lebeau, Vicky. "'You're My Friend': *River's Edge* and Social Spectatorship." *Camera Obscura*, nos. 25–26 (January-May 1991): 251–73.

Lee, Janet. "Subversive Sitcoms: *Roseanne* as Inspiration for Feminist Resistance." *Women's Studies* 21 (1992): 87–101.

Leibman, Nina C. "Leave Mother Out: The Fifties Family in American Television." *Wide Angle* 10 (1988): 24–41.

Lembo, Ronald, and Kenneth H. Tucker. "Culture, Television, and Opposition: Rethinking Cultural Studies." *Critical Studies in Mass Communication* 7, no. 2 (1990): 97–116.

Leo, John. "A Pox on Dan and Murphy." *U.S. News and World Report*, 1 June 1992, 19.

———. "Toxic Feminism on the Big Screen." *U.S. News and World Report*, 10 June 1991, 20.

Lesage, Julia. "Feminist Film Criticism: Theory and Practice." In *Sexual Stratagems: The World of Women in Film*, edited by Patricia Erens, 144–55. New York: Horizon Press, 1979.

———. "The Human Subject—You, He, or Me? (Or, the Case of the Missing Penis)." *Screen* 16 (summer 1975): 77–83.

Lewis, Lisa. "Consumer Girl Culture: How Music Video Appeals to Girls." In *Television and Women's Culture: The Politics of the Popular*, edited by Mary Ellen Brown, 89–101. London: Sage, 1990.

———. *Gender Politics and MTV: Voicing the Difference*. Philadelphia: Temple University Press, 1991.

Lichter, S. Robert, Linda S. Lichter, and Stanley Rothman. "From Lucy to Lacey: TV's Dream Girls." *Public Opinion* 9 (September-October 1986): 16–19.

Lipsitz, George. "The Meaning of Memory: Family, Class, and Ethnicity in Early Network Television Programming." In *Recasting America: Culture and Politics in the Age of Cold War*, edited by Lary May, 79–116. Chicago: University of Chicago Press, 1989.

Long, Elizabeth. *The American Dream and the Popular Novel*. Boston: Routledge and Kegan Paul, 1985.

———. "Feminism and Cultural Studies." *Critical Studies in Mass Communications* 6, no. 1 (1989): 427–35.

———. "Women, Reading, and Cultural Authority: Some Implications of the Audience Perspective in Cultural Studies." *American Quarterly* 38, no. 4 (fall 1986): 591–612.

Lopate, Carol. "Daytime Television: You'll Never Want to Leave Home." *Feminist Studies* 4, no. 6 (1978): 69–82.

Lovell, Terry. *Pictures of Reality: Aesthetics, Politics and Pleasure.* London: British Film Institute, 1980.

MacCabe, Colin, editor. *High Theory/Low Culture: Analyzing Popular Television and Film.* New York: St. Martin's Press, 1986.

MacDonald, J. Fred. *Blacks and White TV: Afro-Americans in Television since 1948.* Chicago: Nelson-Hall, 1983.

Macdonnell, Diane. *Theories of Discourse.* London: Basil Blackwell, 1986.

Mann, Karen. "Narrative Entanglements: *The Terminator.*" *Film Quarterly* 43, no. 2 (winter 1989–90): 17–27.

Marc, David. *Comic Visions: Television Comedy and American Culture.* Winchester, Mass.: Unwin Hyman, 1989.

Mast, Gerald. *A Short History of the Movies.* Indianapolis: Bobbs-Merrill, 1976.

———, editor. *The Movies in Our Midst: Documents in the Cultural History of Film in America.* Chicago: University of Chicago Press, 1982.

Mast, Gerald, and Marshall Cohen, editors. *Film Theory and Criticism.* New York: Oxford University Press, 1979.

Mayerle, Judine. "*Roseanne*—How Did You Get Inside My House? A Case Study of a Hit Blue-Collar Situation Comedy." *Journal of Popular Culture* 24, no. 4 (winter 1991): 71–88.

Mayne, Judith. "The Female Audience and the Feminist Critic." In *Women and Film*, edited by Janet Todd, 22–40. New York: Holmes and Meier, 1988.

———. "*LA Law* and Prime-Time Feminism." *Discourse* 10, no. 2 (spring-summer 1988): 30–47.

———. "Review Essay: Feminist Film Theory and Criticism." *Signs* 11, no. 1 (1985): 81–100.

———. "Visibility and Feminist Film Criticism." *Film Reader*, no. 5 (1980): 120–24.

———. *The Woman at the Keyhole: Feminism and Women's Cinema*. Bloomington: Indiana University Press, 1990.

———. "The Woman at the Keyhole: Women's Cinema and Feminist Criticism." *New German Critique* 23 (1981): 27–43.

McLuhan, Marshall. *Understanding Media: The Extensions of Man*. New York: McGraw-Hill, 1964.

McNeil, Alex. *Total Television*. New York: Penguin, 1980; 2d updated and revised edition, 1991.

McRobbie, Angela. "Postmodernism and Popular Culture." In *Postmodernism*, 54–58. London: ICA, 1986.

McRobbie, Angela, and Jenny Garber. "Girls and Subculture." In *Resistance through Rituals*, edited by Stuart Hall and Tony Jefferson, 209–22. London: Hutchinson, 1976.

Meehan, Diana M. *Ladies of the Evening: Women Characters of Prime-Time Television*. Metuchen, N.J.: Scarecrow Press, 1983.

Meese, Elizabeth. *Crossing the Double-Cross*. Chapel Hill: University of North Carolina Press, 1986.

Mellen, Joan. *Women and Their Sexuality in the New Film*. New York: Horizon Press, 1973.

Mellencamp, Patricia. *Indiscretions: Avant-Garde Film, Video, and Feminism*. Bloomington: University of Indiana Press, 1990.

———, editor. *Logics of Television: Essays in Cultural Criticism*. Bloomington: Indiana University Press, 1990.

Metz, Christian. *Film Language: A Semiotics of the Cinema*. Translated by Michael Taylor. New York: Oxford University Press, 1974.

Miller, Mark Crispin. *Seeing through Movies*. New York: Pantheon, 1990.

Mitchell, Juliet. *Psychoanalysis and Feminism*. Harmondsworth: Penguin, 1975.

Mitchell, Juliet, and Jacqueline Rose, editors. *Feminine Sexuality: Jacques Lacan and the "Ecole Freudienne."* New York: Norton, 1982.

Mitz, Rick. *The Great TV Sitcom Book*. New York: Perigree Books, 1983.

Modleski, Tania. "Femininity as Mas(s)querade: A Feminist Approach to Mass Culture." In *High Theory/Low Culture: Analyzing Popular Television and Film*, edited by Colin MacCabe, 37–52. New York: St. Martin's Press, 1986.

————. *Feminism without Women: Culture and Criticism in a "Postfeminist" Age*. New York: Routledge, 1991.

————. *Loving with a Vengeance: Mass-Produced Fantasies for Women*. New York: Methuen, 1982.

————. *The Women Who Knew Too Much: Hitchcock and Feminist Theory*. New York: Routledge, 1988.

————, editor. *Studies in Entertainment: Critical Approaches to Mass Culture*. Bloomington: Indiana University Press, 1986.

Moi, Toril. *Sexual/Textual Politics: Feminist Literary Theory*. London: Methuen, 1985.

Moore, Suzanne. "Here's Looking at You, Kid!" In *The Female Gaze: Women as Viewers of Popular Culture*, edited by Lorraine Gamman and Margaret Marshment, 44–59. London: The Women's Press, 1988.

Moores, Shaun. "Texts, Readers and Contexts of Reading: Developments in the Study of Media Audiences." *Media, Culture and Society* 12 (1990): 9–29.

Morgan, Robin, editor. *Sisterhood Is Powerful: An Anthology of Writings from the Women's Liberation Movement*. New York: Vintage Books/Random House, 1970.

Morley, David. *Family Television: Cultural Power and Domestic Leisure*. London: Comedia, 1986.

————. *Television, Audiences and Cultural Studies*. London: Routledge, 1992.

Morris, Meaghan. "Banality in Cultural Studies." In *Logics of Television: Essays in Cultural Criticism*, edited by Patricia Mellencamp, 14–43. Bloomington: Indiana University Press, 1990.

Mulvey, Laura. "Afterthoughts on 'Visual Pleasure and Narrative Cinema' . . . Inspired by *Duel in the Sun*." *Framework* 15/16/17 (1981): 3–10. Reprinted in Laura Mulvey, *Visual and*

Other Pleasures, 29–38, Bloomington: Indiana University Press, 1989.

———. "British Film Theory's Female Spectators: Presence and Absence." *Camera Obscura*, nos. 20–21 (May-September 1989): 68–81.

———. *Visual and Other Pleasures*. Bloomington: Indiana University Press, 1989.

———. "Visual Pleasure and Narrative Cinema." *Screen* 16 (1975): 6–18. Reprinted in *Popular Television and Film*, edited by Tony Bennett, Susan Boyd-Bowman, Colin Mercer, and Janet Woollacott, 12–15, London: British Film Institute with the Open University Press, 1981.

Murdock, Graham. "Cultural Studies at the Crossroads." *Australian Journal of Communication* 16 (December 1989): 37–49.

Murdock, Graham, and Peter Golding. "Capitalism, Communication and Class Relations." In *Mass Communication and Society*, edited by James Curran, Michael Gurevitch, and Janet Woollacott, 12–43. London: Sage, 1979.

National Organization for Women. *Women in the Wasteland Fight Back: A Report on the Image of Women Portrayed in TV Programming*. Washington, D.C.: National Organization for Women, National Capitol Area, 1972.

Neale, Steve. "Questions of Genre." *Screen* 31, no. 1 (spring 1990): 45–66.

Nelson, Cary, and Lawrence Grossberg, editors. *Marxism and the Interpretation of Culture*. Urbana: University of Illinois Press, 1988.

Newcomb, Horace, editor. *Television: The Critical View*. Oxford: Oxford University Press, 1976.

Newton, Judith, and Deborah Rosenfelt, editors. *Feminist Criticism and Social Change: Sex, Class and Race in Literature and Culture*. New York: Methuen, 1985.

Nichols, Bill. *Ideology and the Image*. Bloomington: Indiana University Press, 1981.

————, editor. *Movies and Methods*. Berkeley and Los Angeles: University of California Press, 1976.

Nochimson, Martha. *No End to Her: Soap Opera and the Female Subject*. Berkeley and Los Angeles: University of California Press, 1992.

Nochlin, Linda. *Women, Art, and Power and Other Essays*. New York: Harper and Row, 1988.

Novak, Robert. "*Thelma and Louise*." *People Weekly*, 10 June 1991, 18.

O'Connor, John. *American History/American Television*. New York: Frederick Ungar, 1983.

Ohmer, Susan. "Measuring Desire: George Gallup and Audience Research in Hollywood." *Journal of Film and Video* 43, nos. 1–2 (1991): 3–28.

Oshana, Maryann. "Native American Women in Westerns: Reality and Myth." *Film Reader* 5 (1982): 125–31.

Owens, Craig. "The Discourse of Others: Feminists and Postmodernism." In *The Anti-Aesthetic: Essays on Postmodern Culture*, edited by Hal Foster, 57–82. Port Townsend, Wash.: Bay Press, 1983.

Pall, Ellen. "In Sitcoms, Cupid Is Often Only a Tease." *New York Times*, 28 January 1990, 31.

Parenti, Michael. *Inventing Reality: The Politics of the Mass Media*. New York: St. Martin's Press, 1986.

Parker, Rozsika, and Griselda Pollock, editors. *Framing Feminism: Art and the Women's Movement 1970–1985*. London: Pandora Press, 1987.

Penley, Constance. "Feminism, Psychoanalysis, and the Study of Popular Culture." In *Cultural Studies*, edited by Lawrence Grossberg, Cary Nelson, and Paula Treichler, 479–500. New York: Routledge, 1992.

————. "The Lady Doesn't Vanish: Feminism and Film Theory." In *Feminism and Film Theory*, edited by Constance Penley, 1–24. New York: Routledge, 1988.

————, editor. *Feminism and Film Theory*. New York: Routledge, 1988.

Perkins, T. E. "Rethinking Stereotypes." In *Ideology and Cultural Production*, edited by Michele Barrett, Philip Corrigan, Annette Kuhn, and Janet Wolff, 135–59. New York: St. Martin's Press, 1979.

Pollock, Griselda. "What's Wrong with Images of Women?" *Screen* 24 (autumn 1977): 25–33.

Poster, Mark. *The Mode of Information: Poststructuralism and Social Context*. Chicago: University of Chicago Press, 1990.

Postman, Neil. *Amusing Ourselves to Death: Public Discourse in the Age of Show Business*. New York: Viking Penguin, 1985.

Press, Andrea. *Women Watching Television: Gender, Class, and Generation in the American Television Experience*. Philadelphia: University of Pennsylvania Press, 1991.

Pribram, E. Deidre, editor. *Female Spectators: Looking at Film and Television*. London: Verso, 1988.

Probyn, Elspeth. "Feminism and Cultural Studies." *Canadian Journal of Political and Social Theory* 11, nos. 1–2 (1987): 139–43.

Przybylowicz, Donna. "Toward a Feminist Cultural Criticism: Hegemony and Modes of Social Division." *Cultural Critique* 19 (winter 1989–90): 259–301.

Rabinowitz, Dorothy. "Politics as Usual in Hollywood." *Wall Street Journal*, 21 September 1992, A10.

Rabinowitz, Paula. "Review Essay: Seeing through the Gendered I: Feminist Film Theory." *Feminist Studies* 16, no. 1 (spring 1990): 151–69.

Radstone, Susannah. "Woman to Women: Review of *Alice Doesn't.*" *Screen* 26, nos. 3–4 (May 1985): 111–15.

Radway, Janice. "Identifying Ideological Seams: Mass Culture, Analytic Method, and Political Practice." *Communication* 9, no. 1 (1986): 93–123.

———. "Mail-Order Culture and Its Critics: The Book-of-the-Month Club, Commodification and Consumption, and the Problem of Cultural Authority." In *Cultural Studies*, edited by Lawrence Grossberg, Cary Nelson, and Paula Treichler, 512–30. New York: Routledge, 1992.

————. *Reading the Romance: Women, Patriarchy, and Popular Literature*. Chapel Hill: University of North Carolina Press, 1984; with a new introduction by the author, 1991.

————. "Reception Study: Ethnography and the Problems of Dispersed Audiences and Nomadic Subjects." *Cultural Studies* 2, no. 3 (1988): 359–76.

Rakow, Lana F. "Feminist Approaches to Popular Culture: Giving Patriarchy Its Due." *Communication* 9, no. 1 (1986): 19–41.

Rapp, Rayna. "Is the Legacy of Second-Wave Feminism Post-feminism?" In *Women, Class, and the Feminist Imagination: A Socialist-Feminist Reader*, edited by Karen V. Hansen and Ilene J. Philipson, 357–62. Philadelphia: Temple University Press, 1990.

Raymond, Diane, editor. *Sexual Politics and Popular Culture*. Bowling Green, Ohio: Bowling Green State University Popular Press, 1990.

Real, Michael R. *Super Media: A Cultural Studies Approach*. London: Sage, 1989.

Rich, Ruby. "Anti-Porn: Soft Issue, Hard World." *Feminist Review* 3 (February 1983): 56–67.

————. "In the Name of Feminist Film Criticism." In *Issues in Feminist Film Criticism*, edited by Patricia Erens, 268–87. Bloomington: University of Indiana Press, 1990.

Richardson, Kay, and John Corner. "Reading Reception: Mediation and Transparency in Viewers' Accounts of a TV Programme." *Media, Culture and Society* 8 (1986): 485–508.

Roach, Jacqui, and Petal Felix. "Black Looks." In *The Female Gaze: Women as Viewers of Popular Culture*, edited by Lorraine Gamman and Margaret Marshment, 130–42. London: The Women's Press, 1988.

Robinson, John. "He Hates It." *Boston Globe*, 14 June 1991, 29.

Roman, Leslie, Linda Christian-Smith, and Elizabeth Ellsworth. *Becoming Feminine: The Politics of Popular Culture*. Philadelphia: Falmer Press, Taylor and Francis, 1988.

Root, Jane. *Picture of Women: Sexuality*. London: Pandora Press/Routledge and Kegan Paul, 1984.

Rose, Jacqueline. *Sexuality in the Field of Vision*. London: Verso, 1986.

Rosen, Marjorie. *Popcorn Venus*. New York: Avon, 1973.

Rosenburg, Bernard, and David Manning White, editors. *Mass Culture: The Popular Arts in America*. Glencoe, Ill.: Free Press, 1957.

Ross, Andrew. *Universal Abandon? The Politics of Postmodernism*. Minneapolis: University of Minnesota Press, 1988.

Rubey, Dan. "Voguing at the Carnival: Desire and Pleasure on MTV." *South Atlantic Quarterly* 90, no. 4 (fall 1991): 871–906.

Russo, Vito. *The Celluloid Closet: Homosexuality in the Movies*. New York: Harper and Row, 1987.

Rutsky, R. L., and Justin Wyatt. "Serious Pleasures: Cinematic Pleasure and the Notion of Fun." *Cinema Journal* 30, no. 1 (fall 1990): 3–19.

Ryan, Michael, and Douglas Kellner. *Camera Politica: The Politics and Ideology of Contemporary Hollywood Film*. Bloomington: Indiana University Press, 1990.

Schiller, Herbert. *Communication and Cultural Domination*. White Plains, N.Y.: International Arts and Sciences Press, 1976.

Schulze, Laurie. "On the Muscle." In *Fabrications: Costume and the Female Body*, edited by Jane Gaines and Charlotte Herzog, 59–78. New York: Routledge, 1990.

Schwichtenberg, Cathy, editor. *The Madonna Connection*. Boulder: Westview Press, 1993.

Seiter, Ellen. "Feminism and Ideology: The *Terms* of Women's Stereotypes." *Feminist Review* 22 (February 1986): 58–81.

———. "Stereotypes and the Media: A Re-evaluation." *Journal of Communication* 36, no. 2 (spring 1986): 14–26.

Seiter, Ellen, Hans Borchers, Gabriele Kreutzner, and Eva-Maria Warth, editors. *Remote Control: Television, Audiences and Cultural Power*. London: Routledge, 1991.

Sheridan, Susan, editor. *Grafts: Feminist Cultural Criticism*. London: Verso, 1988.

Shoos, Diane. "The Female Subject of Popular Culture." *Hypatia* 7, no. 2 (spring 1992): 215–26.

Showalter, Elaine, editor. *The New Feminist Criticism: Essays on Women, Literature, and Theory*. New York: Pantheon, 1985.

Shrage, Laurie. "Feminist Film Aesthetics: A Contextual Approach." *Hypatia* 5, no. 2 (summer 1990): 137–48.

Silverman, Kaja. *The Acoustic Mirror: The Female Voice in Psychoanalysis and Cinema*. Indianapolis: Indiana University Press, 1988.

———. "Dis-Embodying the Female Voice." In *Re-Vision: Essays in Feminist Film Criticism*, edited by Mary Ann Doane, Patricia Mellencamp, and Linda Williams, 131–49. Los Angeles: American Film Institute, 1984.

———. *The Subject of Semiotics*. New York: Oxford University Press, 1983.

Simon, John. "Movie of the Moment." *National Review*, 8 July 1991, 48–50.

Singer, Linda. "Eye/Mind/Screen: Toward a Phenomenology of Cinematic Scopophilia." *Quarterly Review of Film and Video* 12, no. 3 (1990): 51–67.

Sklar, Robert. *Movie-Made America: A Cultural History of American Movies*. New York: Vintage, 1975.

Sklar, Robert, and Charles Musser, editors. *Resisting Images: Essays on Cinema and History*. Philadelphia: Temple University Press, 1990.

Snortland, Ellen. "'Values' Is Code for 'Dad Is the Boss.'" *Los Angeles Times*, 22 May 1992, B7.

Sochen, June. "The New Woman and Twenties America: Way Down East." In *American History/American Film: Interpreting the Hollywood Image*, edited by John O'Connor and Martin Jackson, 1–15. New York: Frederick Ungar, 1979.

Solinger, Rickie. "Murphy Brown, at the Pinnacle of Choice." *Los Angeles Times*, 17 May 1992, M5.

Sontag, Susan. *A Barthes Reader*. New York: Hill and Wang, 1982.

Spender, Dale, editor. *Men's Studies Modified: The Impact of Fem-*

inism on the Academic Disciplines. New York: Athene Series/Pergamon Press, 1981.

Spigel, Lynn. "Installing the Television Set: Popular Discourses on Television and Domestic Space, 1948–1955." *Camera Obscura* 16 (January 1988): 11–46.

Spigel, Lynn, and Denise Mann. "Women and Consumer Culture: A Selective Bibliography." *Quarterly Review of Film and Video* 11 (1985): 85–105.

———, editors. *Private Screenings: Television and the Female Consumer*. Minneapolis: University of Minnesota Press, 1992.

Spottiswoode, Raymond. *A Grammar of the Film*. Berkeley and Los Angeles: University of California Press, 1962.

Stacey, Jackie. "Desperately Seeking Difference." *Screen* 28 (1987): 48–61.

Stacey, Judith. "Sexism by a Subtler Name? Postindustrial Conditions and Postfeminist Consciousness in Silicon Valley." In *Women, Class, and the Feminist Imagination: A Socialist-Feminist Reader*, edited by Karen V. Hansen and Ilene J. Philipson, 338–56. Philadelphia: Temple University Press, 1990.

Steeves, Leslie H. "Feminist Theories and Media Studies." *Critical Studies in Mass Communication* 4, no. 2 (June 1987): 95–135.

Stern, Leslie. "Feminism and Cinema: Exchanges." *Screen* 20, nos. 3–4 (1979–80): 89–105.

Stimpson, Catharine. *Where the Meanings Are: Feminism and Cultural Spaces*. New York: Routledge, 1989.

Storr, Robert. "The Theoretical Come-On." *Art in America* 74 (April 1986): 158–65.

Studlar, Gaylyn. "Masochism, Masquerade, and the Erotic Metamorphosis of Marlene Dietrich." In *Fabrications: Costume and the Female Body*, edited by Jane Gaines and Charlotte Herzog, 229–49. New York: Routledge, 1990.

Taubin, Amy. "'Cheers' It Ain't: David Lynch Expands the Parameters of Prime Time." *Village Voice*, 10 April 1990, 33–36.

Taylor, Ella. *Prime-Time Families: Television Culture in Postwar*

America. Berkeley and Los Angeles: University of California Press, 1989.

Todd, Janet, editor. *Women and Film*. New York: Holmes and Meier, 1988.

Torres, Sasha. "Melodrama, Masculinity and the Family: *thirtysomething* as Therapy." *Camera Obscura* 19 (January 1989): 87–107.

Traube, Elizabeth G. *Dreaming Identities: Class, Gender, and Generation in 1980s Hollywood Movies*. Boulder: Westview Press, 1992.

Tuchman, Gaye. "Introduction: The Symbolic Annihilation of Women by the Mass Media." In *Hearth and Home: Images of Women in the Mass Media*, edited by Gaye Tuchman, Arlene Kaplan Daniels, and James Benet, 3–38. New York: Oxford University Press, 1978.

———. "The Newspaper as a Social Movement's Resource." In *Hearth and Home: Images of Women in the Mass Media*, edited by Gaye Tuchman, Arlene Kaplan Daniels, and James Benet, 186–215. New York: Oxford University Press, 1978.

Tuchman, Gaye, Arlene Kaplan Daniels, and James Benet, editors. *Hearth and Home: Images of Women in the Mass Media*. New York: Oxford University Press, 1978.

Turim, Maureen. "Fashion Shapes: Film, the Fashion Industry, and the Image of Women." *Socialist Review* 71 (September-October): 83–95.

———. "Gentlemen Consume Blondes." *Wide Angle* 1, no. 1 (1980): 52–59.

Turner, Bryan, editor. *Theories of Modernity and Postmodernity*. London: Sage, 1990.

Turner, Graeme. *Film as Social Practice*. London: Routledge, 1990.

Tyler, Parker. *Screening the Sexes: Homosexuality in the Movies*. Garden City, N.Y.: Anchor, 1973.

United States Commission on Civil Rights. *Window Dressing on the Set: Women and Minorities in Television*. Washington, D.C.: U.S. Government Printing Office, 1977.

Walker, Janet. "Hollywood, Freud and the Representation of Women: Regulation and Contradiction, 1945–early 60s." In *Home Is Where the Heart Is: Studies in Melodrama and the Woman's Film*, edited by Christine Gledhill, 197–214. London: British Film Institute, 1980.

Wallace, Michele. *Invisibility Blues: From Pop to Theory*. London: Verso, 1990.

Waller, Gregory, editor. *American Horrors: Essays on the Modern American Horror Film*. Chicago: University of Illinois Press, 1987.

Walsh, Andrea. *Women's Films and Female Experience, 1940–1950*. New York: Praeger, 1984.

Walters, Suzanna Danuta. *Lives Together/Worlds Apart: Mothers and Daughters in Popular Culture*. Berkeley and Los Angeles: University of California Press, 1992.

———. "Material Girls: Feminism and Cultural Studies." *Current Perspectives in Social Theory* 12 (1992): 59–96.

Wartella, Ellen, and Paula A. Treichler. "Interventions: Feminist Theory and Communication Studies." *Communication* 9, no. 1 (1986): 1–18.

Weedon, Chris. *Feminist Practice and Post-Structuralist Theory*. Oxford: Basil Blackwell, 1987.

Weiss, Andrea. "'A Queer Feeling When I Look at You'—Hollywood Stars and Lesbian Spectatorship in the 1930s." In *Stardom: Industry of Desire*, edited by Christine Gledhill, 293–99. London: Routledge, 1991.

West, Cornel. "The New Politics of Difference." *October* (summer 1990): 93–109.

White, Diane. "She Loves It." *Boston Globe*, 14 June 1991, 29.

White, Susan. "With Regard to Female Spectatorship." *Quarterly Review of Film and Video* 12, no. 4 (1991): 93–105.

Whitehead, Barbara Dafoe. "What Is Murphy Brown Saying? For Starters, That Unwed Motherhood Is a Glamorous Option." *Washington Post*, 10 May 1992, C5.

Wiggins, A. *Sex Role Stereotyping: A Content Analysis of Radio and Television Programs and Advertisements*. Vancouver: National Watch on Images of Women in the Media, 1985.

Williams, Linda. "Feminist Film Theory: *Mildred Pierce* and the Second World War." In *Female Spectators: Looking at Film and Television*, edited by E. Deidre Pribram, 12–30. London: Verso, 1988.

———. *Hard Core: Power, Pleasure and the Frenzy of the Visible*. Berkeley and Los Angeles: University of California Press, 1989.

———. "Something Else besides a Mother: *Stella Dallas* and the Maternal Melodrama." In *Home Is Where the Heart Is: Studies in Melodrama and the Woman's Film*, edited by Christine Gledhill, 299–325. London: British Film Institute, 1987.

Williams, Raymond. *Communications*. 3d edition. New York: Penguin, 1976.

———. *Culture*. Glasgow, United Kingdom: Fontana Press, 1981.

———. *Culture and Society*. New York: Harper and Row, 1958.

———. *Keywords: A Vocabulary of Culture and Society*. New York: Oxford University Press, 1976.

———. *Marxism and Literature*. Oxford: Oxford University Press, 1977.

———. *Problems in Materialism and Culture*. London: Verso, 1980.

———. *Television: Technology and Cultural Form*. New York: Schocken, 1975.

Williamson, Judith. *Consuming Passions: The Dynamics of Popular Culture*. London: Marion Boyars, 1986.

———. *Decoding Advertisements: Ideology and Meaning in Advertising*. London: Marion Boyars, 1978.

———. "The Problems of Being Popular." *New Socialist* (September 1986): 14–15.

———. "Woman Is an Island: Femininity and Colonization." In *Studies in Entertainment: Critical Approaches to Mass Culture*, edited by Tania Modleski, 99–118. Bloomington: Indiana University Press, 1986.

Willis, Paul. *Common Culture*. Boulder: Westview Press, 1990.

————. *Profane Culture*. London: Routledge and Kegan Paul, 1978.

Willis, Sharon. "Hardware and Hardbodies: What Do Women Really Want? A Reading of *Thelma and Louise*." In *Film Theory Goes to the Movies*, edited by Jim Collins, Hilary Radner, and Ava Preacher Collins, 120–28. New York: Routledge, 1993.

————. "Special Effects: Sexual and Social Difference in *Wild at Heart*." *Camera Obscura*, nos. 25–26 (January-May 1991): 275–95.

Winship, Janice. "Handling Sex." In *Looking On: Images of Femininity in the Visual Arts and Media*, edited by Rosemary Betterton, 25–39. London: Pandora Press, 1987.

Wollen, Peter. *Signs and Meaning in the Cinema*. London: Secker and Warburg/British Film Institute, 1972.

"Women and Film: A Discussion of Feminist Aesthetics." *New German Critique* 13 (winter 1978): 83–107.

Women and Film. *What's Wrong with This Picture?* Research report, in collaboration with the National Commission on Working Women. Washington, D.C.: Women and Film, 1990.

Wood, Robin. *Hollywood from Vietnam to Reagan*. New York: Columbia University Press, 1986.

Woolf, Janet. *The Social Production of Art*. New York: New York University Press, 1981.

Wright, Will. *Sixguns and Society: A Structural Study of the Western*. Berkeley and Los Angeles: University of California Press, 1975.

Yang, J. E., and A. Devroy. "Quayle: 'Hollywood Doesn't Get It.'" *Washington Post*, 21 May 1992, A1, A17.

Young, Shelagh. "Feminism and the Politics of Power: Whose Gaze Is It Anyway?" In *The Female Gaze: Women as Viewers of Popular Culture*, edited by Lorraine Gamman and Margaret Marshment, 173–88. London: The Women's Press, 1988.

Zeck, Shari. "Female Bonding in *Cagney and Lacey*." *Journal of Popular Culture* 23 (winter 1989): 143–54.

Index

Compositor:	Integrated Composition Systems
Text:	11/14 Aster
Display:	Aster
Printer and binder:	Edwards Bros.